Other Symbols

⅄ delete

X obvious error

∧ omission

√ good point; interesting idea

A CONCISE GUIDE FOR WRITERS

Louis E. Glorfeld
University of Denver

David A. Lauerman
Canisius College, Buffalo

Norman C. Stageberg
University of Northern Iowa

A CONCISE GUIDE FOR WRITERS

FOURTH EDITION

Holt, Rinehart and Winston
New York Chicago San Francisco
Atlanta Dallas Montreal Toronto
London Sydney

Library of Congress Cataloging in Publication Data

Glorfeld, Louis E
A concise guide for writers.

Includes index.
   1. English language—Rhetoric.   I. Lauerman, David A., joint author.
II. Stageberg, Norman C., joint author   III. Title.
PE1408.G56   1977   808'.042   77–23236

First ed. published in 1963 under title: A concise guide for student writers.

ISBN: 0–03–018801–6

7 8 9 0   065   9 8 7 6 5 4 3 2 1

To the Instructor

This fourth edition of *A Concise Guide for Writers* has a number of changes. We have added two new chapters—one on the research paper, the other on the resume and application letter—and two new entries in Section 2: connotation and subjunctive. We have also added an appendix on the parts of speech. In addition, we have increased the number of revision-practice sentences and updated topical material. The overall goal of this brief textbook remains the same: to aid the student-writer to achieve a simple and clear writing style.

Section 1 offers the student practical hints on getting started and suggests a strategy for outlining and drafting short themes.

Section 2 takes up the more common writing faults, one at a time. A brief and simple explanation is given for each fault, with ample illustrations drawn from student writing. Meticulous qualifications and overrefinements are avoided. Following the explanations, two sets of revision exercises are presented; each set consists of sentences taken mostly from themes written by freshmen that embody the fault with which the explanation is concerned. Thus the student, by grappling with real, not factitious, writing problems, has the sense of performing a task that will bring a welcome reward—success in the mastery of one important step toward sound writing.

Section 3 deals with broader problems that face the beginning writer. The first two chapters cover sentence flow and thought development. The next two chapters present the procedures and techniques of outlining and of preparing a simple research paper. These are followed by a chapter on writing essay examinations; this chapter is perhaps most profitably taught shortly before the fresh-man students face their first mid-term examinations. Finally, there is a brief chapter on two writing tasks that are of vital concern to many students: the resume and job-application letter. The appendix on the parts of speech is intended for instructors who find it con-venient in teaching composition to have this knowledge readily available to students.

We should emphasize that this guidebook is neither a grammer nor a complete handbook of composition. Rather, it contains a thoughtful selection of those writing problems that college freshmen need most help with. We have learned, through using the guide in the classroom ourselves, that its economy of presentation is helpful in clarifying difficulties for students.

The instructor may use the guide in several ways: (1) Use the correction symbols for written work, thus referring each student to the explanations and exercises needed. (2) Assign the pages dealing with those faults that are causing difficulties for the class as a whole. (3) Teach the material in the book in the order in which it appears, with original written work at intervals.

• • •

We are grateful to the following for their help on this fourth edition of *A Concise Guide for Writers*: Ron Arias, Crafton Hills College, Yucaipa, California; Christine Barabas, George Williams

College, Downers Grove, Illinois; Paul T. Bryant, Colorado State University; James R. Canterbury, Evergreen Valley College, San Jose, California; Vincent Gillespie, Kansas State University; Kathleen A. Hart, Bowling Green State University; Michael Joyce, Jackson Community College, Jackson, Michigan; Jan Mackie, Stephens College, Columbia, Missouri; Alfred McDowell, Bergen Community College, Paramus, New Jersey; Richard Pepp, Massasoit Community College, Brockton, Massachusetts; Roberta L. Thibault, Onondaga Community College, Syracuse; Daryl Troyer, El Paso Community College; Harender Vasudeva, Bowling Green State University. We are grateful also to Richard F. Somer of Denver for his assistance on the research paper chapter. We wish to express particular appreciation to Richard S. Beal of Boston University for his constructive critique of the manuscript.

L.E.G.
D.A.L.
N.C.S.

Denver, Colorado
Buffalo, New York
Cedar Falls, Iowa

December, 1976

CONTENTS

A CONCISE GUIDE FOR WRITERS

1
GETTING READY TO WRITE

WRITING IS THINKING

We all enjoy talking—telling about what we have done, what we are thinking, what made us laugh or made us feel uneasy. Talking gives us a chance to look back over events and feelings, put them in words, and see how our friends react to them. After talking things over, we feel as if we have thought things out. For a lot of us, talking is thinking.

When we write, the same sort of process goes on, and we end up with the same sort of satisfaction. We look back over our store of experiences, ideas, and feelings and frame them in words. Afterwards, we feel better—satisfied that our ideas have taken shape. Writing is thinking.

Talking and writing are both thinking, but we all know that there are differences between the two. These differences mean that sometimes it takes a while to find the satisfaction that comes from writing. As we settle down to talk with friends, we see familiar faces and we hear immediate reactions. As we settle down to write, we see nothing but a blank sheet of paper. That makes us uneasy. We may have disturbing thoughts like these: How can I start a conversation with a blank sheet of paper? But I have to begin, somehow, if I am going to enjoy this. I must begin to think. I must begin to write.

Begin where? Most people who write well have learned some trick for getting started. First, of course, they begin to *think* about the topic they have in mind. But then comes the trick—the way they begin to *write*. Some people start by jotting down word doodles; some write introductions; some make lists of ideas; some sit down to write only after they have the opening sentence all worked out mentally. These methods have one thing in common: all are ways of getting some *words* onto the blank paper. When they work, they produce what every writer needs—notes on paper that are connected in some way with a topic. The first big hurdle has been crossed. The next thing to do is to search among these notes for a handle on the topic —a way to deal with the topic. In finding the handle, the writer looks for several items of information relating to the topic, a plan for arranging these items, and an opening sentence or approach.

Getting words onto paper, finding a handle, making a plan—all these are part of "Getting Ready to Write," the subject of Section 1 of this book. We've been talking pretty much in generalities so far, but now we will get down to cases. The rest of this section presents a specific writing strategy—one that has helped many students to get their thoughts into writing. We begin at the beginning, with a trick for getting started.

A Trick for Getting Started

The procedure involves several simple steps. (1) Spend a few minutes jotting down quickly whatever thoughts come to mind. For this brief period it is important to *keep writing*. Things that seem trivial at first become helpful as they awaken further words and ideas. These written thoughts become a set of notes that will be the basis of your paper. (2) Sort these notes into groups that seem to go together. The trick here is to find general items that include other items. The item that is the most general one of all may become the overall subject of your discussion. You may reject items that do not fit or that seem unimportant. (3) Arrange the groups in some sensible order. (4) Take a second look at the grouped items. Fill in gaps and cross out items that don't fit. You now have a scratch outline to work with. More important, you have done some thinking in two stages and you are ready to write. (5) Write the first draft of the paper rapidly, making few or no changes or corrections as you go. Pay attention only to the flow of your ideas. When this is finished, you have a rough draft. You are on your way.

A WRITING STRATEGY

Now we will go through the process in greater detail, following what one student did. Janet has been asked to write about some accomplishment that she is especially proud of. She does not know yet what she'll say. Still, she tries to relax and begins to jot down the first things that come into her head:

Making a shirt for Tom.
Getting an A on the psych mid-term exam.
My car was a rusty wreck. But now it's not so bad.
Fixing it up. Still not finished.
Myriad scratches and dents.
New parts: fender and grill. Motor OK.

Janet has something in writing. She did not try to say anything in particular, you'll notice. So far, she is letting the words that come to mind flow freely onto the page. But now there is a pattern to be seen in her notes. She has found a tentative subject—fixing her car—and she begins to focus her attention on extending her list on that subject:

1. My car was a rusty wreck. But now it's not so bad.
2. Fixing it up. Still not finished.
3. Myriad scratches and dents.
4. New parts: fender and grill. Motor OK.
5. An 11-year-old Ford (Mustang).
6. Needed fender, grill, lights (possibly a whole new front end).
7. Parts from junk yard.
8. Money (ran out of money).
9. First the filler, then the sanding, then the priming, last the paint.
10. Used Dad's garage and tools (and some help!).
11. Still not painted: ran out of money.
12. Still don't have my Dream Car.

Janet has listed more than ten points, and she has found a topic that fits the assignment: "I am proud of fixing my car." (That's also a tentative statement of her main idea.) Now if she can sort these items into two or three groups, she'll have plenty of material for a three-paragraph theme.

Janet's second task is to sort things out and start combining. She looks through the list for similar items. Items 4, 7, 8, and 10 seem to be related: they list the main things she needed to fix up her car:

NEEDS
Fender, grill, lights.
Parts from junk yard.
Money (ran out of money).
Used Dad's garage and tools (and some help!).

Similarly, Janet connects items 1, 3, and 6. These items list some of the things wrong with her car:

PROBLEMS
My car was a rusty wreck. But now it's not so bad.
Myriad scratches and dents.
Had to find fender, grill, headlights.

The remaining items don't make a neat set, but item 9 has to do with the steps in the repair process, and items 2 and 11 seem somewhat related. Janet decides to try this arrangement:

PROCESS

Fixing it up. Still not finished.
First the filler, then the sanding, then the priming, last the paint.
Still not painted: ran out of money.

That list doesn't satisfy Janet. She decides to use the sequence within item 9 to describe the repair process:

REPAIR PROCESS

First, sand the rust off.
Fill in the holes and sand the filler; repeat several times.
Prime the shiny spots.
Professional paint job (still not done).

This is not a very tidy outline. For one thing, you will note that Janet did not include items 5 and 12 anywhere on her lists. Those items aren't lost; they'll be kept at hand for later use. The first hasty list has served its purpose: it has kept her writing and thinking.

A three-paragraph theme is taking shape as Janet turns to the third step—working out a sensible order for arranging these three groups. That needn't take long. She has noticed that one of the groups describes her *Problems*. That is a sensible place to begin. And the *Process* of doing the actual repairs can't begin until after her *Needs* for parts and tools are taken care of. That adds up to a sensible arrangement: *Problems–Needs–Process*. Other logical sequences may occur to us, but Janet is wise enough to keep working with what she has.

Janet goes on to step four. She makes a readable copy of her scratch outline. As she copies the items in order, she changes wording, fills in other details as they come to mind, eliminates the overlap between items 2 and 11 ("still not finished"), and finds a home for item 5 (under *Problems*). Also, she decides how to use item 12: it supplies her with a title.

MY DREAM CAR

1. Problems with my old car:
   a. My 11-year-old Mustang was a wreck.
   b. It was covered with rust, scratches, and dents, and the paint was bad.
   c. Needed a whole new front end: fender, grill, lights.

2. What I needed to fix it up:
   a. A 1966 Mustang with a good front end.
   b. Some new parts from a junkyard and materials: filler, sandpaper, primer.
   c. Money for parts, materials, and the paint job.
   d. Garage and tools (and help).
3. The repair process:
   a. First, sand the rust off.
   b. Fill in the holes and sand the filler; repeat several times.
   c. Prime the shiny spots.
   d. Get a professional paint job (still not done).

If Janet paused for so much as a drink of water at this point, her grasp of these ideas might dribble away. She immediately begins writing a thesis sentence. The general subject is fixing her car; the sentence also has to state that she took pride in fixing it. That's enough for a tentative opening:

I am especially proud of having fixed up my old 1966 Mustang.

That sentence may be changed later on, but Janet doesn't pause: she watches as the words of her first draft flow across the page.

MY DREAM CAR

I am especially proud of having fixed up my old 1966 Mustang. After a myriad of major and minor accidents I decided that, for the sake of my neighborhood and for my own personal satisfaction, I would either have to replace the car or repair it. But due to an acute shortage of money I was forced to keep what I had and fix it up. The first thing I did was to evaluate my *problem*. It was rusty, there were small scratches, still deeper gouges and the paint was bad. A front fender, grill and lights that simply had to be replaced. The only asset the car had left was that it was completely dependable as far as the engine was concerned and thats what I needed a car that would always start.

The next step was to round up parts and materials. I was on my 9th yard before I found a car identical to mine and somewhat intact, the problem being in finding a car that was over 11 years old in that particular make and model, even in a junkyard. The remainder of the body parts I would have to buy, along with lots of body filler and primer. Luckily my Dad does a lot of body work, so I had plenty of tools and free advice available.

After replacing the parts that I could find the remaining scratches and gouges had to be repaired with body filler. The process is relatively simple but time consuming. It involves filling the damaged areas with prepared filler, sanding it down and repeating the process, as much as five times for the more severely damaged areas. After this step was finished

I spot primed the entire car. I am planning to have it professionally painted this fall or wait till spring, the only delaying factor being the money problem mentioned earlier. When the entire process is finished I hope to have the new looking car I've always dreamed of.

Now Janet may sit back, as she would after a pleasant hour of conversation, and feel the pleasure that comes of having said what she wanted to say. Of course this is still very rough copy, and much polishing remains to be done. After working for a while at something else, Janet will return to begin polishing her work. She will have to change words and revise sentences, tidy up spelling and punctuation, and consult her dictionary. When she has finished and the result looks good, she will set her paper aside to cool. Next day, she will reread it: in the light of morning the flaws will stand out more clearly for correction. At last she will copy the final version. For Janet, writing is thinking. It's not easy, but it can be satisfying.

Sharpening the Thesis Sentence

Janet's first draft was easier to write because she followed a clear writing strategy. She arranged the elements in the repair process in step-by-step order, and she developed a tentative thesis sentence. This sentence stated her controlling idea:

I am especially proud of having fixed up my old 1966 Mustang.

Janet was able to go on writing paragraph after paragraph by following her outline and staying within the limits of this thesis sentence. And anyone reading Janet's paper later on may use that sentence as a guide to Janet's purpose in writing the paper. Thus Janet's revised paper should begin with her thesis sentence. Furthermore, Janet will begin the process of revising her paper by revising the thesis sentence.

Remember, a thesis sentence indicates the writer's purpose. Such a statement of purpose is not found in all kinds of writing, but it is useful to the writer and the reader when both want to be particularly clear about the substance and purpose of the information presented. It is useful in all college writing—most especially in writing papers and essay exams. Keep in mind also that the thesis sentence should do two things: (1) Since it is in effect a summary of the writer's main idea, it should state the general subject of the paper. (2) Since it states the writer's opinion or ideas, it should describe the particular, special aspect of the general subject which the writer chooses to discuss here and now. (Incidentally, a thesis is sometimes expressed in two or more sentences, but it works best when it is a single sentence.)

Janet places her tentative thesis sentence at the beginning of the paper:

I am especially proud of having fixed up my old 1966 Mustang.

Whatever follows this thesis sentence should be connected to it and should fall within the limits of the subject which it states. But Janet now sees a problem in its design. The general subject—"fixing up my car"—is at the end of the sentence, and Janet's opinion is at the beginning: "I am especially proud . . . ." Inverting the order produces a more direct thesis sentence:

Fixing up my old 1966 Mustang made me especially proud.

This form has the advantage of stating first the general subject, then the opinion. It will be a clear and useful guide in the revision work that follows.

Suppose Janet had decided to write on one of the other topics that occurred to her. Consider her first idea—"Making a shirt for Tom." Those words describe the general subject. Janet was given the rest of the thesis sentence as part of the writing assignment: doing this "made me very proud." These elements combine into a thesis sentence: "Making a shirt for Tom made me very proud." Had she chosen to write on that topic, Janet could have used that thesis sentence both in developing her outline and again later on in revising her draft.

Some More Examples

Let's take another look at writing strategies. Here are some topics of the kind often handed out to college freshmen at the beginning of the fall semester:

First impressions of the campus
Women in college athletics
Why I decided to return to college
The advantages of a community college over a large university
The disadvantages of working while going to college
What makes a really good teacher

Which one would you choose as the topic for a three-paragraph theme? Anyone could write on the first topic. For the second and third, you need to have some specific impressions in mind; if you have some experience with either of those, choose the one that comes closer to you. The last three direct you to a specific approach to the topic given; they require you to support what you say. You will choose one of these if some supportive ideas come to mind and if you feel that you can think of others.

Suppose we work up the first topic—"First Impressions of the Campus." All you need do in this case is ask yourself, "What was it like?" and begin your list of notes:

a weird experience
like wandering into a new part of town
independence!
noise and crowds
missing classes
different people
making out my own schedule
people sleeping in class
like starting a new job
the teachers are older
crowded bookstore and cafeteria

Given such a broad topic, you may find it hard to stop making notes. However, you already have several key points and can begin arranging them. One method would be to arrange the points chronologically, beginning with your arrival on campus and ending with your first class. Another would be to list your impressions under headings, in this manner:

I. A weird experience: noise and crowds, like a new part of town . . .
II. Independence: choosing teachers, missing classes . . .
III. New routine: bookstore, cafeteria, teachers, classes . . .

Using this set of headings, you can prune away subjects that do not fit in, and you may be reminded of others that do relate to the three headings. Now you can go ahead and arrange your scratch outline.

A slightly different approach is needed for a topic such as "The Advantages of a Community College over a Large University." To make a clear and convincing statement on this topic, you will need to point out both the advantages and disadvantages of each, and you will list topics with this purpose in mind:

THE COMMUNITY COLLEGE
small campus, friendly
close to home

low tuition
familiar faces and places
limited choice of teachers and courses

THE LARGE UNIVERSITY
large campus, not as friendly as small campus
over 100 miles from home; too far
expenses of tuition, dorm, and travel
strange city and new faces; hard to get acquainted
great variety of courses and professors

You will note that this first list has at least one shortcoming. It is heavily biased in favor of the community college. If you want to show your reader that you are fair-minded, you should list additional disadvantages of the community college and additional advantages of the large university. But if you actually wish to emphasize the advantages of the community college to your reader, the topics must be rearranged so that these advantages are the last things mentioned in your paper. The strategy you choose for selecting and arranging the ideas you offer will help to determine your reader's acceptance of them.

Happily, after their first few themes, most students no longer face the problem of getting started. As you, too, become comfortable with the process, you'll enjoy it; writing will become easier for you, and you will no longer need to fear that blank sheet of paper.

EXERCISES

1. Produce a list of items, a scratch outline, and the thesis sentence for one of the topics in the list on page 9.
2. Here is a final revised revision of the theme entitled, "My Dream Car." Compare it with the first draft and be able to explain in class why the revisions have been made.

MY DREAM CAR
Fixing up my old 1966 Mustang made me especially proud. I've always dreamed of having a nice-looking car, but the money it would take to buy one always stopped me. So last summer I decided to take a different approach and patch up the body on my 11-year-old Mustang. I took a good long look at the car and decided that what I had was a wreck. It was rusty and covered with small scratches and deep gouges. The paint was bad. One front fender and the grill and lights were com-

pletely shot. The only good feature left on the whole car was that the engine was in perfect condition.

The first step was to buy a lot of sandpaper, body filler, and primer. The next step was to round up the body parts in area wrecking yards. I had a hard time finding a car that was 11 years old in that particular make and model, even in a junk yard. I was on my ninth yard before I found a car identical to mine and somewhat intact. Paying for the fender, grill, and headlights used up the last of my money. Luckily my father does a lot of body work, so I had plenty of tools and free advice available.

Replacing the fender and grill and lights took lots of time and help from my dad. Next, working by myself, I smoothed out all the scratches and gouges. It was a slow process—filling the damaged areas with prepared filler, sanding them down, and repeating the process as many as five times. After that I primed the shiny areas. I am planning to have the entire car repainted next spring when I get some more money saved. Then I'll have the car I've always dreamed of.

2 OVERCOMING HIGH-FREQUENCY FAULTS

1·AP
ACTIVE AND PASSIVE

An active verb is one whose subject is the doer of the action, as in

Our neighbor *stole* the boat.

The author *discussed* the nature of literature.

The manager will *close* the restaurant at nine.

In these examples the verbs are active because the doers of the action are the subjects *neighbor, author,* and *manager.*

A passive verb consists of at least two parts: a form of *be (am, is, are, was, were, be, been)* and a past participle, as in *is stolen, are stolen, had been stolen, was discussed, will be closed.* Here is a sentence with a passive verb:

The boat had been stolen.

Note that the doer is not mentioned. To tell your reader who/what the doer is in a passive verb sentence, you must add a *by* phrase, thus:

The boat had been stolen by our neighbor.

To use the passive effectively, you should be aware of two warnings:

1a. Avoid "weak passives"—those that do not serve a purpose. These only lead to wordy constructions and false emphasis. Here are some examples:

The biggest fish were caught by me and my brother.

The next topic has already been discussed by my opponent.

I was surprised to hear the view that was expressed by him.

These sentences are neither wrong nor unclear, but they would sound more straightforward if they were made active:

My brother and I caught the biggest fish.

My opponent has already discussed the next topic.

I was surprised to hear the view he expressed.

1b. A sentence that begins in the active voice should not be shifted to the passive voice without good reason. Take this sentence, for example:

The speaker who does this believes that he is correct in the point which is being put across.

It would be more natural and direct to retain the active voice throughout:

The speaker who does this believes that he is correct in the point which he is trying to put across.

The passive voice is a convenient rhetorical device that may be effectively used in at least four situations:

2a. When the writer wishes to remain noncommittal:

We suspected that the boat had been stolen.

Here the writer remains uncommitted as to who did the stealing.

2b. When a link with the preceding sentence is needed:

This is one definition of literature. *The other* has already been discussed.

In this construction, *other* is placed close to its referent, *definition,* in order to aid the flow of ideas.

2c. When the doer is unimportant:

The restaurant will be closed at nine.

2d. When the subject of a passive verb is the matter of greatest interest:

A lovely red Persian rug was unrolled at our feet.

REVISION PRACTICE

Identify and correct active-passive shifts and "weak passives" in the following sentences:

1. In writing a report, the writer should limit himself to observed facts, and care must be taken not to include opinions and judgments.
2. I was able to finish the first semester, but a lot of adjustments had to be made.
3. Once the lesson was studied and the paper written, plans were made for an exciting weekend.

4. When paddling a canoe across a rough lake, great care must be taken to avoid tipping.
5. At every performance of the symphony, the music was enjoyed by me more.
6. Melody wanted to be warm enough on the ski trip. After she bundled up in her woolen skirt and ski sweater, her long scarf was found and put on.

ADDITIONAL REVISION PRACTICE

Identify and correct active-passive shifts and "weak passives" in the following sentences:

1. Archery can be participated in by any number of people.
2. While one is taking the trouble to solve one difficulty, another is noticed.
3. We sent them information, and ideas were exchanged in a spirit of warmth and cooperation.
4. The reviews on this new and popular play were disagreed with by the theater audiences.
5. He was handed his discharge by the president of the company.
6. She drove the car skillfully. After looking in both directions for cars, the gear was shifted, after which the clutch was released slowly and she was on her way.

2 · Agr SV
AGREEMENT OF SUBJECT AND VERB

To understand the agreement of subject and verb, let us first look at the forms of the present tense of a regular English verb. Here they are:

Person	Singular	Plural
1st	I work	we work
2nd	you work	you work
3rd	he works	they work

Of these six verb forms, one is out of line—*works*. It has an *-s* ending that is not shared by the others. This *-s* form is used when the subject is any singular pronoun except *I* and *you,* as in

He works.

She plays.

It depends.

Each prefers his own instrument.

Each of the musicians *prefers* his own instrument.

Everyone wishes to aid the ethnic minorities.

Neither believes he is wrong.

Neither of the debaters *believes* he is wrong.

The *-s* form of the verb is also used when the subject is a singular noun; for example,

His *duty depends* on his orders.

A *mistake occurs* in the second chapter.

A *mistake* in punctuation mechanics *occurs* in the second chapter.

The same *-s* ending is also the ending of irregular verb forms—*is, was, has, does*—all of which occur with a singular subject in the third person, as in

My favorite *activity is* tennis.

The main *thing was* the wieners.

Her *calf has* won the prize.

Each does his best.

Everybody was asked to bring refreshments.

Now, if we look again at the six verb forms at the beginning of this paragraph, we note that the plural forms, in the right-hand column, are simply the bare verb without any ending—*work*. Verb forms without endings are the ones used with plural subjects in the present. Here are some examples:

The young *people work.*

The young *people* in the volunteer groups *work* hard.

Jack, Susan, and *Harry come* late to class on Tuesdays.

His *duties depend* on his orders.

The *duties* of the chairman *seem* simple.

Many go to the auditorium lectures.

The plural form *are,* which is irregular in form, also takes a plural subject, as in

These *activities are* time-consuming.

The *activities* offered by our junior college *are* time-consuming.

All are standing in the hall.

All this is simple, and you probably have already learned not to write *they was,* or *it depend,* or *the student have.* But there are five special sentence situations in which you are liable to go wrong in your singulars and plurals. We will illustrate all five:

1. A troublesome situation is this:

The *duties* of the guard *depends* on the type of post.

You know that the plural *duties* requires the plural form of the verb, *depend;* and you would naturally say *duties depend.* But the intervening modifier, *of the guard* (in which the noun is singular), lures you into a singular form of the verb, *depends.* To avoid this kind of error, put your one-word subject together with its verb and see if they match; the subject-verb *duties depends* is obviously a mismating; hence you must shift to *duties depend.*

2. Another sentence situation that causes singular-plural trouble is the *which-who-that* clause. This sentence will show the trouble:

My roommate has two thoroughbred *calves* on his father's farm which *has* won several prizes at the Cattle Congress.

The difficulty is that, in this kind of sentence, the verb is often distant from the governing subject, so that the writer forgets what number he should use for the verb. To test this situation, simply put the subject, relative, and verb together—*calves* which *has*—and you will see at once that the verb should be *have.*

3. Another troublesome situation may be illustrated by this sentence:

For me the most important thing in high school *were* the activities.

Here the plural word *activities* has coaxed a plural verb out of you, but it is the word before the verb, *thing,* that is the subject, and your sentence should read:

For me the most important *thing* in high school *was* the activities.

If, however, you made *activities* the subject, then the sentence would read:

For me *activities were* the most important thing in high school.

4. A trouble spot occurs in the *there* type of sentence, where the subject follows the verb. Be cautious with *there;* it is merely a "function" word that gets the sentence started:

In the new gym there *is* a swimming *pool*, a wrestling *room*, and a basketball *court.*

With a plural subject—*pool, room,* and *court*—a plural verb is needed:

In the new gym there *are* a swimming *pool*, a wrestling *room*, and a basketball *court.*

Here is the same kind of error in another sentence:

In tennis there *occurs* several *mistakes* that beginners should avoid.

Since the subject, *mistakes,* is plural, it should have a plural verb:

In tennis there *occur* several *mistakes* that beginners should avoid.

5. The final difficulty in agreement occurs when a collective noun is the subject of the verb. A collective noun is the name of a collection of persons or things, such as *audience, band, chorus, class, club, combo, committee, congregation, crowd, group, family, remainder, team.*

When you use a collective noun as the subject to mean the collection as a whole, you use a singular verb with it:

The congregation was singing the last hymn softly.

After each meeting, the committee issues its minutes.

But when you mean the individuals of the collection, you use a plural verb:

The congregation were dropping coins on the collection plate.

The committee have disagreed.

Sometimes either the singular or the plural form of the verb will be appropriate:

The crowd has been shouting excitedly.

The crowd have been shouting excitedly.

REVISION PRACTICE

Revise these sentences, correcting errors in agreement.

1. Each of his many friends have listed his positive traits.
2. While we remained, everything that belonged to the members of our group were there for the use of all of us.
3. The objectives of the program, of which I was fully informed, has made me less eager to become a member.
4. Over by the fireplace was two chairs.
5. There was only a table and a chair on the stage for the first act.
6. Neither of these two things are true of college life.
7. The results I expect to obtain from my education is equal to the amount of effort expended.
8. Each of the chapters stress a different problem.
9. There is in the lounge a new oil painting and an 18th-century engraving.
10. There's many students who have not read their booklet on college regulations.

ADDITIONAL REVISION PRACTICE

Revise these sentences, correcting errors in agreement.

1. Every one of the candidates are under eighteen.
2. Neither of the girls are a good choice.
3. The thickness of the wrestling mats vary.
4. Each of the guards have a particular job to do.
5. In our society today there exists many problems that can be solved only by social scientists.
6. Learning the rudiments of music are not difficult.
7. Among the guests was an artist, a ball player, a writer, and a bank president.
8. The law of averages protect you in a risky situation such as thi.
9. Any one of these people are capable of doing the work.
10. In his studio there is a large easel, a potter's wheel, and a tub of dry clay.

3 · Amb
AMBIGUITY

A word or passage is ambiguous when it can convey more than one meaning to the reader. Sometimes an ambiguity occurs because two meanings of a single word can be understood in a given context. Here is an example:

I'll do that in an hour.

The writer, who probably thought this sentence seemed simple, direct, and clear, did not notice that the word *in* can convey two meanings here, so that the sentence can mean either

I'll do that within an hour.

or

I'll do that after an hour.

This type of ambiguity, stemming from the multiple meanings of individual words, is called lexical ambiguity.

A second type is syntactic ambiguity. This is occasioned by the grammatical arrangement of words. Here are a few of the many arrangements that may produce syntactic ambiguity:

1. Adjective + noun + noun, as in

heavy hog production.

In this example, the adjective *heavy* can modify either *hog*, with the resultant meaning of "production of heavy hogs"; or the noun phrase *hog production,* giving a meaning of "hog production that is heavy." The ambiguity can be removed by a hyphen, thus

heavy-hog production

heavy hog-production

2. *More* + adjective + noun, as in

Give more realistic details.

This sentence can mean either "Give details that are more realistic" or "Give more details that are realistic."

3. Adjective + series of nouns, as in

A baseball player must have good vision, coordination, and speed.

In this sentence, the adjective *good* may modify either *vision* alone or the whole series—*vision, coordination,* and *speed*. We can remove the ambiguity by these revisions:

A baseball player must have sharp vision, coordination, and speed.

A baseball player must have coordination, speed, and good vision.

4. Head + modifier + head. The term *head* refers to the word modified. In this arrangement the modifier may modify either the preceding or the following word, as in

What we believe profoundly influences our ability to listen fairly.

Here we cannot tell whether the writer means "believe profoundly" or "profoundly influences." The ambiguity can be corrected by changing the position of *profoundly,* thus:

What we profoundly believe influences our ability to listen fairly.

What we believe influences profoundly our ability to listen fairly.

A qualification about ambiguity must be made. A sentence that is ambiguous in isolation will sometimes be clear in a controlling context. For example,

She appealed to him

by itself has two meanings: (1) She was attractive to him; (2) She requested him (for something or to do something). But it is clear in these contexts:

With her wavy golden hair and sky-blue eyes, she appealed to him in a way that made him wish to know her better.

She appealed to him for mercy.

Ambiguities are elusive. When your mind is fixed on one meaning it is sometimes very difficult to make a mental shift to the other meaning. Therefore your instructor may wish to devote class time to locating the double meaning of each sentence before you begin revising the sentences below. But if the instructor does not care to do this, you will find it helpful to work with a fellow student in order to locate the ambiguities.

REVISION PRACTICE (Lexical Ambiguities)

Revise each sentence so as to remove the ambiguity and present one meaning clearly.

1. *How* will he find his dog tomorrow?
2. Mac's sister did not *care for* the pigeons.
3. She *rented* the house for $250 a month.
4. The agents *collect* at the drug store.
5. My family has moved around a great deal, and in twelve years of schooling I have had thirty *odd* teachers.
6. Our milk has a *stable* flavor the year around.
7. For just $10 a year you can read *about* 3,000 books a year. (Advertisement)
8. Foreign ladies have *fits* upstairs. (Sign above the entrance of a two-story tailor shop in Hong Kong)
9. Mac is my *oldest* friend.
10. The campaigners are *revolting*.

REVISION PRACTICE (Syntactic Ambiguities)

Revise each sentence so as to remove the ambiguity and present one meaning clearly.

1. Businessmen who are afraid to take risks frequently lose out to their competitors.
2. The club needed more intelligent officers.
3. In last night's paper I read a clever reporter's story.
4. This salve offers soothing relief for mild sunburn, poison oak, and poison ivy.
5. My roommate insisted on wearing a big plaid shirt.
6. In my methods course we studied modern language teaching.
7. This laboratory needs more up-to-date equipment.
8. The club will be open to members only from Monday to Thursday.
9. I took out for an afternoon's sail my sister Patricia, her English tutor, Cecilia Reilly, and a classmate from Millbrook.
10. Steve lived six months after the operation, which was longer than the doctor expected.

4 · Cap and LC
CAPITALIZATION AND LOWER CASE

The use of capital letters is a matter of either style or convention. In situations where writers make a stylistic choice, they should be governed by the need for clarity and emphasis. For example, good writers often capitalize such words as *Church, State, Hope, Truth,* or *the Presidency* when they are referring to concepts important within the context of their writing (rather than simply using the word in a general sense). Writers may capitalize almost any noun (*Reproduction, Redundancy, Management, Labor*) to indicate that it is a key word. But be wary of these uses of capital letters.

Many of the conventions, such as capitalizing the first word of a sentence, the pronoun *I,* and pronouns referring to God, are so familiar as to need little explanation. In the following situations, however, inexperienced writers often forget to capitalize:

1. In titles, the first and last words and every word except articles, prepositions, and conjunctions are capitalized.* Freshman writers often allow the shortness of a word to mislead them. Here are some typical errors in titles:

   Faulty   Explaining the signs of the Zodiac
   Correct Explaining the Signs of the Zodiac

   Faulty   The Attrition rate of College Freshmen
   Correct The Attrition Rate of College Freshmen

   Faulty   The Challenges And Difficulties of my new Position
   Correct The Challenges and Difficulties of My New Position

2. The words *east, west, south, north* or combinations of these are capitalized when they refer to sections of the country, but they are not capitalized when they indicate directions. You would capitalize *west* in this sentence—

---

* Examples of these three parts of speech are: (1) Articles: *the, a, an.* (2) Prepositions: *of, in, from, with, about, between, to.* (3) Conjunctions: *and, but, since, as, if, when, though.* In titles, many people follow a widely accepted modification: they capitalize prepositions and conjunctions that have five or more letters.

I learned about the old West from watching TV.

but not in this one—

You go west two blocks to reach the junction.

3. Months and days of the week are always capitalized:

In August the regular Tuesday meetings were canceled.

4. Titles of persons in high office and personal names are capitalized. You should capitalize here—

Tonight I am going to hear the Senator from Minnesota.

Did you hear Senator Humphrey?

but not here—

My brother is no longer a company president.

Elizabeth is the president of the freshman class.

5. A word designating a family relationship (like *cousin, mother, uncle*) is capitalized when it precedes a personal name. We write, "My uncle was ill," but "We adored Uncle Bill." Here is an example:

> Faulty   The house has a big front porch where grandmother and grandfather Jones sit every night after supper.
> Correct The house has a big front porch where Grandmother and Grandfather Jones sit every night after supper.

6. A word designating a family relationship is capitalized when it is used instead of a personal name. We write, "I introduced my mother to the professor," but "I told Mother that I was going out." Here are some examples:

> Faulty   George is like dad, but I am like mother.
> Correct George is like Dad, but I am like Mother.

> Faulty   My Father and my Mother run a store together.
> Correct My father and my mother run a store together.

7. Names of races, nationalities, and languages are always capitalized.*

In our neighborhood a group of Italians and Jews have set up a nursery school.

---

* Exception: *blacks* and *whites*. Example: "The blacks and whites paraded together for better housing."

We went to a restaurant that featured Chinese food.

The Indians all spoke good English.

8. Generic names, such as *zinnia, winter, college,* are not capitalized, but specific names are, for example, *Red Giant Zinnias, Easter, Grinnell College.*

9. College subjects, such as *biology, psychology, mathematics, literature,* are not capitalized, except for cases like *American history* and *French literature.* But specific course titles are capitalized, for example, *Fundamentals of Biology II, Psychology 240, Mathematics for General Education, Afro-American Literature.*

REVISION PRACTICE

Revise the following sentences, correcting any mistakes in capitalization that you find.

1. When I found they were open, I immediately registered for history 220 and biology 106.
2. Their debate topic last year was this: "Should Auxiliary Solar Heating Be Required for All New Housing?"
3. He first came to the northwest early in his career and later settled permanently in the east.
4. In Autumn life was dull indeed but Spring was a different matter.
5. She is a mythical maiden from the area now called the holy land.
6. Joan enjoyed reading about the history of china.
7. After labor day he no longer felt the urge to go north on fishing trips.
8. Uncle Fred had given him the watch on the tuesday before he had graduated from Mt. Morris high school.
9. Most College Graduates have little difficulty in finding jobs in this field.
10. Nobody read professor Harold's book unless forced to read it.

ADDITIONAL REVISION PRACTICE

Correct any mistakes in capitalization that you find.

1. My roommate has trouble with Mathematics and Statistics, but not with Literature and Foreign Languages.

2. She was window-shopping on Madison avenue.
3. The activities he enjoyed were Debating and Dramatics.
4. I have one tough course this semester, latin-american civilization.
5. His theme had the title "That Government is best Which Governs Least."
6. The excellence of football in the South is being challenged by the southwest.
7. Her Pansies were not the happy smiler variety.
8. Look up these words in the American College Dictionary as well as in Webster's new collegiate dictionary.
9. Alice Swenson was elected the Secretary of the junior class.
10. My aunt Jane and my Mother are sisters.

5 · Cl
CLICHÉ

A cliché (pronounced *clee-sháy*) is an expression that has been overused so much that it no longer has any vividness or punch. A good example is *as strong as an ox*. Long ago, when the ox bending to the plow in the fields was a common sight, this expression must have conveyed a vivid impression of power. But today, used and heard by people who have never seen an ox, it is flat and stale. Our language is filled with clichés. They are handy counters in the give-and-take of ordinary conversation but have little place in careful, written prose. Here are a few, which will doubtless recall many others to your mind: *as old as the hills, stood like a sentinel, as bald as a billiard ball, last but not least, sadder but wiser, age before beauty, as brown as a berry.*

The remedy for a cliché is to substitute fresh and vigorous words that will vividly indicate what you wish to convey. Why say *as brown as a berry?* How many berries can you think of that are brown? Instead, why not say something less hackneyed, such as *brown as an autumn oak leaf, brown as a coconut, brown as a Hereford,* or *brown as cinnamon?*

Another way to replace a cliché is to use a simple and direct expression. For *pull down a victory*, use *win*. For *rears its ugly head*, use *appears* or *presents itself*.

REVISION PRACTICE

In revising the following sentences, try to strengthen them by using fresh, imaginative expressions or simple direct terms instead of clichés.

1. Where else could you find out that you are not entering a cold, cruel world?
2. To many students the lagoon is a place where one can get away from the hustle and bustle of campus activities.
3. People trying to save money will do without this or that and never go overboard on anything.
4. His idea does not hold too much ground in the twentieth century.
5. I view with alarm this surprising development.

ADDITIONAL REVISION PRACTICE

In revising the following sentences, try to strengthen them by using fresh, imaginative expressions or simple, direct terms instead of clichés.

1. Last but not least, I learned that life is not cut and dried.
2. Chances are that truer words have never been spoken.
3. His better half rules the roost.
4. Being around so many extroverts brought her out of her shell.
5. Getting money from my roommate was like pulling teeth.

6 · Clq
COLLOQUIAL

A colloquial expression is one that is popular and acceptable in conversation and informal writing, but is not used in formal writing. A few familiar examples of colloquialisms are *kind of* (rather), *a lot, fizzle out, goner, mighty* (as in *mighty pleased*), *awful* (as in *awful glad*), *go back on,* and *real* (as in *real good*). Since a rather formal style is required for most college themes and papers, you should avoid colloquial terms in such writing.

Your desk dictionary will help you with usage problems like this one. Three of the desk dictionaries usually recommended for college students label these terms *Colloq.* or *Slang.* A fourth recommended dictionary, *Webster's New Collegiate,* does not use either of these labels, apparently in the belief that the status of such terms cannot be accurately ascertained. There are occasionally differences among the three dictionaries in their choice of usage labels; for instance, a word labeled *Colloq.* in one may be classified as *Slang* in another. In either case, the word indicated should not be used in formal writing.

You must also remember that a usage label often applies only to a specific use of a word, not to all of its meanings. The word *comeback,* for example, has three definitions in one desk dictionary. One of these is standard usage, the second is slang, and the third is colloquial.

See also **38 Sl** and **22 NS.**

7 · Col
USES OF THE COLON

The uses of the colon are easy to understand.
   1. Like the dash, it is used to signal to the reader that a series or list will follow:

   During our January sale we are featuring the following items: boys' T-shirts, shorts, and socks; men's slacks and underwear; and ladies' raincoats, hats, and overshoes.

It is often regarded as poor practice to separate the main elements of a sentence—subject, verb, and object—by a colon:

   We saw: battleships, cruisers, carriers, and destroyers.

You will notice immediately that the colon separating the verb from the object is unnecessary:

   We saw battleships, cruisers, carriers, and destroyers.

However, in a long, more fully developed sentence, this use of the colon can be helpful:

   After the first attack had subsided and we had had several hours to rest, the chief gunner reported: three battleships, all accompanied by escort vessels; thirteen troop carriers; an undetermined number of aircraft carriers, all of which seemed to have planes at the ready; innumerable PT boats.

2. The colon indicates that the next clause to come will clarify, expand, or illustrate the idea just mentioned. Here are some examples:

There is no time for love: we are doomed.

To deny this is to deny the basic premise of the Declaration of Independence: "All men are created equal."

I had seen her before, so I knew what to expect: she was all skin and bones.

3. The colon serves the same purpose in introducing a long quotation:

He made these interesting comments concerning the character of Iago in *Othello:*

Iago seems to be the enemy of love. In fact, he seems to be the enemy of all emotion. He spins ruthlessly a web of jealousy in the mind of Othello.

REVISION PRACTICE

Provide a colon where appropriate in the following sentences. Rewrite when necessary.

1. For actors of today I know some other excellent advice Hamlet's speech to the players.
2. This is the reason we are returning to humanism because the world situation requires it, not because man is improving his character.
3. The question is this. Should we agree to settling problems such as these in such a haphazard and selfish manner?
4. He had one idea in his head to get out of the room at once and in a socially acceptable manner.
5. One is asked for the following types of themes. They are definition, description, comparison, and clarification.
6. For your next assignment please read an article from one of the following magazines *Harper's, The Atlantic, Scientific American,* or the *Saturday Review.*

ADDITIONAL REVISION PRACTICE

Provide a colon where appropriate in the following sentences. Rewrite when necessary.

1. He had three diverse hobbies stamp collecting, swimming, and drag racing.
2. He had a very good reason for not coming to the party he was not invited.
3. The main question is this. Should the examination be uniform throughout the United States, or should it be so constructed as to fit the problems peculiar to each state?
4. Creon thus summarized the theme of Oedipus the King "Do not seek to be master in everything, for the things you master will not follow you throughout your life."
5. There was also the social purpose to meet students from different areas.

8 · C
USES OF THE COMMA

More than 80 percent of the punctuation marks used inside the sentence are commas. Hence it is important that you master the uses of the comma if you are to guide your reader accurately along the trail of your thoughts. The dictum that a writer uses commas to represent slight pauses is useful, but you will do better to learn to apply the simple set of rules given below. These rules, together with those explained under **10 CC** and **28 P Mod,** will enable you to handle most cases of comma-punctuation that will come up in your theme writing. Commas are used:

1. To set apart interrupters, such as words, phrases, or clauses that interrupt the flow of thought.

   He is, by and large, the wealthiest farmer in the country.

   Jim, while a congenial fellow, is not qualified for the position.

2. To separate long introductory phrases and clauses from the rest of the sentence.

Since no athletic scholarships are offered to any students of any university in the conference, the teams deserve to be called amateur.

At a point near the heart of the business district in an ugly little town, the robbery was committed in broad daylight.

3. To separate the main clause from a long clause or phrase that follows it, if the two are separated by a pause or break.

The outcome of the voting had been predicted, although student polling had not been done with any noticeable degree of enthusiasm.

It had been done before, the problem remaining the same each time anyone had tackled it.

4. To separate two long independent or main clauses joined by a conjunction: *and, but, or, for, yet, nor.*

All the city west of the river lay under a blanket of fog, and this made it impossible for traffic to move in any direction the rest of the night.

I can't account for my actions on this particular day, but I know that I was not in the vicinity of the parking lot near the river.

5. To separate items in a series.

He needed new tires, a new muffler, and a new battery for his car.

We looked in the closet, under the bed, and in all the drawers.

When dealing with adjectives in a series, you must distinguish two kinds of situations. If each adjective relates directly to the following noun, then apply the rule above.

a square, two-story, colonial house

But if each adjective seems to modify everything that follows, and the phrase is read smoothly without pauses, do not use commas.

a big old friendly house

Notice that this phrase is read without pauses.

6. To set off *yes* and *no.*

Yes, I can come early if you wish.

No, she has not been informed of the vacancy.

7. To set off words of address.

Bring me the book, Harriet.

I told you, Jim, that you might not be able to finish on time.

8. To separate the names of geographical locations where one location is included within the boundaries of the other.

Claremont, California, is my home.

The license plate indicated that he was from Cook County, Illinois.

The community college in Moline, Illinois, has a good reputation.

9. To separate the date of the month from the year. (A comma between a month alone and the year is optional.)

The family flew from Paris on May 19, 1976, for New York.

He became a citizen in June, [or no comma] 1975.

10. To set off titles and degrees from preceding names.

He was listed as Jackson Holbrook, Jr., in the directory.

The name of the new staff member appeared on the program as Alleen Nilsen, Ph.D.

For the use of commas with restrictive and nonrestrictive modifiers of nouns, see **28 P Mod.**

REVISION PRACTICE

Punctuate the following sentences.

1. It was not necessary in my opinion to advise her to take such a heavy schedule.
2. The main speaker while his talk was pertinent and informative encroached on the time that had been set aside for entertainment.
3. I mentioned it earlier Jerry and had not expected you to bring the subject up again.

4. In a sheltered spot at a place near the road's end the body was hidden.

5. Joe had made the announcement earlier in the evening in front of all his friends but it was embarrassing to him to realize that practically no one wished him well.

6. It however was not a matter of concern to one but to all.

7. I explained to you John and to you Larry that one more revision was absolutely necessary.

8. On November 11 1918 the first war ended and everyone thought it was the war to end all wars.

9. She has read such novels as *Moby Dick The Brothers Karamazov Magister Ludi* and *The Magic Mountain.*

10. After rumors of foul play had been circulated he felt in this instance it was necessary to give out all the information he had.

ADDITIONAL REVISION PRACTICE

Punctuate the following sentences.

1. She had acquired at the auction a set of unmatched dishes a gone-with-the-wind lamp a tea cart some old books and some very bad paintings.

2. They had moved from Little Rock Arkansas to Galveston Texas all in a matter of weeks.

3. She had a list which included such items as clothespins detergent clothes basket clothesline and dye.

4. Yes it is quite likely that he will be elected to the student senate.

5. After dinner had been served and all the guests had been seated in the living room the readings began.

6. Franklin Townsend Jr. spent a life of misery in the town where he was born.

7. If however he had made it very clear in the beginning to all who had shown an interest in the project that they would be substantially rewarded he would not be in the difficulty that he is in now.

8. He had called for loyalty sacrifice and the good old college spirit and yes he had convinced them that these things were necessary for a winning team.

9 · CF
COMMA FAULT OR COMMA SPLICE

1. A *comma fault* (or *comma splice*) is the use of a comma at the end of a word-group where you should have a period, question mark, or semicolon. Here is an example:

This may require as many as ten interviews, however, the client should leave each interview with a feeling of satisfaction.

This sentence, as you can readily see, is confusing to the reader the first time through. It should have been punctuated:

This may require as many as ten interviews; however, the client should leave each interview with a feeling of satisfaction.

or

This may require as many as ten interviews. However, the client should leave each interview with a feeling of satisfaction.

or

This may require as many as ten interviews, however. The client should leave each interview with a feeling of satisfaction.

With this punctuation the writer has guided the reader to the intended meaning.

EXERCISE (1)

Use a period and a capital letter to remove the comma faults from these sentences.

1. The cracked paddle was a handicap in the race, nevertheless they came in a close second.
2. The lightning cracked and large branches were blown down, she had never seen a worse thunderstorm.
3. First he unlocked the trunk, then he got out the jack to raise the back wheels.
4. The book store closed at six o'clock, they had only six minutes to get there.

5. Jane raised her head from the table and began studying again, it seemed stupid to stop when she was almost finished.

2. The next example also has a comma fault, but this one requires a different revision:

Dick was hurt, he won't be able to play.

The best way to revise it is to show the relationship between the two parts (see **41 Sub**) by putting one in a dependent clause:

As Dick was hurt, he was unable to play.

EXERCISE (2)

Use a subordinating conjunction (*although, if, since, while, because*) to remove the comma faults from these sentences.

1. Ralph's bicycle was a good three-speeder, he insisted on having a British ten-speeder.
2. Josephine had studied hard for the exam, she hoped to get a high grade.
3. The boys made the fire, the girls prepared the lunch on the picnic table.
4. Harry was absent from class, he had worked till four A.M. the night before.
5. You go and get a new battery, I'll work on the carburetor.

3. There is still another way to revise comma faults, as we see in the next example:

College has finally begun, about two weeks have gone by.

In cases like this, you can connect the two clauses with a simple conjunction (see **13 Cd**) like *and, but, for, or, yet, nor:*

College has finally begun, and about two weeks have gone by.

EXERCISE (3)

Use a coordinating conjunction (*and, but, yet, so*) to remove the comma faults from these sentences.

1. George's favorite subject was business, Ann preferred art history.
2. The front door was locked, the curtains were drawn tight.

3. His injured back was paining him, he did not attempt to lift the bookcase.
4. Helen waited patiently in her room, the phone never rang.
5. The water boy brought a bottle of liniment, the trainer unwound the elastic bandage.

REVISION PRACTICE

Correct the comma faults you find in these passages.

1. We use many more Anglo-Saxon words than words of Latin or Greek, you will notice they are short, useful, necessary words.
2. There is one instance where I disagree with Ruskin, this is where he suggests going back to the life of the "rustic."
3. Around twelve o'clock I went down to lunch, I have long since forgotten what we had.
4. It is difficult to get interested in the subject, there are also times when one has no time for it.
5. The plane did not prove successful, however, the Germans perfected what the Italians had invented.
6. After the ball game, they attended the dance, they had forgotten to tell their parents about these plans.
7. I miss the sun and the sea, I haven't adjusted to being back.

ADDITIONAL REVISION PRACTICE

Correct the comma faults you find in these passages.

1. The whistle blew, and I tried a reverse, my reverse failed, and I ended up flat on my back.
2. It had rained and frozen the night before, therefore, the trip we had planned seemed risky.
3. Federal Aviation Administration regulations require that the airlines demonstrate their ability to evacuate a fully loaded jetliner in less than 120 seconds, finding up to 250 volunteers to leap from an airplane into the dark has become a problem.
4. I soon began to learn where certain buildings were and where my classes would be held, knowing these things gave me a bit more confidence.
5. She had finished the sketch the day before, she was therefore clearly ready to enter it in the contest.

10 · CC
COMMAS FOR CLEARNESS

A comma will often help your readers avoid misreading your sentence. It will show them which words are grouped together and will indicate where they should pause. Sometimes, for lack of a comma, the reader will misread momentarily and then discover the mistake and have to read the passage again. Here is an example of such momentary confusion caused by the lack of a comma:

About two weeks before I had started to work.

In this sentence readers bump into the period with a shock. Then they reread and discover that *before* is grouped with *about two weeks* and that there is a slight pause following *before*. A comma would have avoided all this trouble:

About two weeks before, I had started to work.

REVISION PRACTICE
Insert the commas that will help the reader to avoid misreading.

1. After we had finished the books were returned to the library.
2. The room itself is small and empty boxes take up most of its area.
3. Jerry passed the cigars to everyone but her father did not seem to approve.
4. When the speaker is moving people are not likely to leave the lecture hall early.
5. After landing the plane caught fire.

ADDITIONAL REVISION PRACTICE
Insert the commas that will help the reader to avoid misreading.

1. Since the quantity is an unknown science has adopted the symbol X.
2. In much the same way a man may decide he should delay marriage until later in life.
3. The house he liked best was near the shopping center and Clear Lake to the south was only minutes away.

4. As a young man dating was my favorite form of relaxation.

5. About three miles beyond the service station can supply you with gas.

11 · Conf
CONFUSED SENTENCE

The term *confused sentence* is a cover-all label that your instructor will use for sentences that are muddled and disorderly, with their parts inserted helter-skelter. There is no single way to go about revising such sentences (see **25 Paral, 41 Sub,** and **23 OBS**). Often, however, one or more of these procedures will be of help to you: (1) take a deep breath and make a new beginning; (2) rearrange the parts; (3) use two or three sentences instead of one. Let us examine this confused sentence:

> In a rural school there is usually no basement, poorly kept floors, outmoded equipment, poor heating, and the floors are extremely drafty in winter.

Now notice what has been done to make this readable:

> Rural schools are in poor condition. They usually have no basement, their equipment is outmoded, and the heating is inadequate. Their floors are poorly kept and are extremely drafty in winter.

Here is another:

> In shorthand you learn the grammar parts of letters about paragraphs, commas, colons, and other punctuation.

This can be simply and directly stated:

> In shorthand you learn two aspects of letter writing—paragraphing and punctuation.

REVISION PRACTICE

Rewrite these sentences to make them orderly and clear.

1. He could be found in the morning at two o'clock in a little gas station on weekends.

2. My sentimental thoughts are of my hometown. It is a very small town out in the middle of the country and all of the farms.

3. In a study of this type emotions would eventually enter, no longer making the study objective.

4. The divisions of freshman English coincide so that some of each division is done at the same time, such as essay reading and theme writing.

5. The marshals usually dressed in red fighting to keep the huge crowds back that line the fairways, all waiting for a chance to see their hero or the tournament leader.

ADDITIONAL REVISION PRACTICE

Rewrite these sentences to make them orderly and clear.

1. Intramural sports play a very important part in every college curriculum through building sportsmanship and also teaching and learning the games to individuals for the enjoyment of the sport.

2. The amazing thing about some of these advertisements, that people just hate and could throw a shoe through the television screen or toss the radio out of the window, do succeed in selling their product.

3. My mother informed me I was an unhappy girl according to Miss Smith and asked that my mother if at all possible have me quit my job.

4. The third, and an important, step is selecting the right kind of tools and equipment. Suggestions will probably be found in seed catalogs, with regard to the types of plants, and an experienced gardener is always free with advice. The gardener must keep in mind the size of the garden. . . .

5. In high school, extracurricular activities were both during class hours and after school. This idea of class and after-school activities gave the student a full schedule and showed the student how to fulfill it in many ways as becoming well acquainted with the activity, becoming active in the activity and give the students the full cooperation to the activity when having meetings or group activities which fall into the extracurricular activity.

12 · Cn
CONNOTATION

Two words you should understand are *denotation* and its partner, *connotation*. Denotation is the agreed-upon sense of a word—what it refers to, stands for, or designates. For example, the word *brink* has the denotation of edge or verge. Connotation is what a word suggests, including attitude, which is normally favorable, neutral, or unfavorable. For instance, *brink* suggests or connotes danger, as in "the brink of a cliff" or "the brink of disaster." Thus, if you write that "Henry was on the brink of receiving his bachelor's degree," the denotation would be right but the connotation would be wrong.

In English we have many sets of words, the members of which have the same denotation but different connotations. For example, if your roommate is very careful about spending money, you might term him *thrifty*, with its favorable connotation. But if you disapprove of this characteristic of his, you could call him *stingy*, with its unfavorable connotation.

Consider for a moment a set of words with the denotation of "not fat." In the trio *slender, thin, skinny*, the connotations are, in order, favorable, neutral, unfavorable. In addition, you have a choice of others with roughly the same denotation, words such as *trim, svelte, willowy, slight, scrawny, lean, lanky, spare, gaunt, stringy*. Since each has, at least in part, the meaning of "not fat," your problem in describing a nonfat person here is to choose the word with just the right connotation. Which ones, for example, would be most appropriate to apply to (a) an attractive girl, (b) an old prospector, (c) a hard-riding cowboy?

If a word you use in a theme is marked **Cn**, you may have a problem in understanding your mistake for these reasons:

(1) Your dictionary may not help you because dictionaries concentrate on denotation and do not often indicate connotation. For an example, look up *brink* in a desk dictionary. (2) The connotation of any word may vary with individuals. Take, for instance, the word *water*. For most of us this has a neutral connotation. But for a girl who has had many pleasurable experiences with water—swimming, canoeing, water-skiing, sailing—*water* will have favorable connota-

tions. And for a girl whose experiences with water have been unpleasant, who cannot swim and who once almost drowned when a boat tipped over, *water* may have unfavorable connotations. (3) The same word may have different connotations in different contexts. Consider, for example, the word *homemade*. In "homemade strawberry jam," *homemade* has a favorable connotation for most, but in "a homemade jacket" the connotation is probably unfavorable, despite the fact that homemade jackets can be skillfully and beautifully crafted.

So, if you are confronted with a **Cn** and your dictionary provides no help, your best procedure is to ask around among your friends to see what connotation they attach to the word in question. If this doesn't work, ask your instructor, who is there to help you.

EXERCISE

In the following sentences, label the words in parentheses as favorable, neutral, or unfavorable by placing the symbol **F, N,** or **U** over each word.

1. My brother is very (cocky self-confident).
2. When she entered the room, a faint (scent smell) accompanied her.
3. Pepe was the most (daring reckless) driver in the stock-car race.
4. My Aunt Polly is always (curious nosey) about neighborhood affairs.
5. Father's lawyer in the case had always been (firm stubborn) in his legal opinions.
6. The witness has a reputation for being (generous wasteful) with his money.
7. Brindlehof achieved (notoriety fame) by his defense of draft evaders.
8. Do you like Caroline's (casual sloppy) way of dressing?
9. We overheard a (quarrel disagreement squabble spat) between the couple in the next apartment.
10. The ties that Dominique wears are invariably (loud colorful flashy gay).

ADDITIONAL EXERCISE

Here is a group of words whose denotations lie in the broad area of "possessing knowledge and using one's mind with skill." Be prepared to discuss in class the connotation of each and to provide an example of the use of each. The words are: *knowledgeable, cunning, intelligent, sly, crafty, learned, well-informed, shrewd, canny, erudite, clever.*

13 · Cd
COORDINATION

Two or more short sentences can sometimes be advantageously combined into one sentence by means of the coordinating conjunctions *and, but, for, or, yet.* Here is an example:

> Beginning a canoe trip at this moment seemed hazardous. The waves were high. The current swirled dangerously between the rocks.

Let us now tie these sentences together by means of coordinating conjunctions:

> Beginning a canoe trip at this moment seemed hazardous, *for* the waves were high, *and* the current swirled dangerously between the rocks.

This use of conjunctions avoids the choppiness of a sequence of short sentences and provides the reader with the thought relationships expressed by the conjunctions. These relationships are:

and	= addition
but, yet	= contrast
for	= reason, cause
or	= alternative choice

In the revised sentence above, *for* shows that the part following is a reason why the trip is considered hazardous, and the *and* indicates that the third part is an additional reason.

When you combine several sentences into one by means of coordinating conjunctions, it is sometimes helpful to change a sentence by omitting or adding words. For example:

> George suddenly braked his bicycle. He turned sharply to the right. He did not want the policeman to see him.

This passage can be easily improved:

George suddenly braked his bicycle and turned sharply to the right, for he did not want the policeman to see him.

Here is another illustration:

Glen worked every evening at the drive-in. He carefully saved his money for seven months. He did not accumulate enough to buy a motorcycle.

In combining these three sentences into one, you will find it helpful to both omit and add words thus:

Glen worked every evening at the drive-in and carefully saved his money for seven months, but even then he did not accumulate enough to buy a motorcycle.

REVISION PRACTICE

Using the coordinating conjunctions *and, but, for, or,* and *yet,* make one sentence out of each group below.

1. He was tall, his figure was muscular. He walked in a springless, flat-footed, and loose-jointed manner.
2. The novel is very interesting. It will probably live for years.
3. Sleeping in a top bunk is dangerous. A fire alarm might sound in the night. This could cause a person to wake up suddenly. He could tumble to the floor.
4. I feel that I have developed a more mature character. At times I am still too intolerant.
5. She pumped the gas pedal. She turned on the starter. The engine would not start.

ADDITIONAL REVISION PRACTICE

Using the coordinating conjunctions *and, but, for, or,* and *yet,* make one sentence out of each group below.

1. The people in the next room are really not inconsiderate. Their talking can distract a student. It makes him feel like telling them to be quiet.
2. Good study habits are useful. Without them a student will learn less in more time.
3. The squirrel did not emerge. He had been frightened by the hunters.
4. Ruth loved to play the clarinet. She practiced only mornings. Then the house was empty.

5. We made considerable progress in clearing out the under-brush. Much more remains to be done. Many trees need to be cut down.

See **41 Sub** for other ways of rewriting a series of short sentences.

14 · DM
DANGLING MODIFIER

A modifier is often placed at the beginning of a sentence. The following sentences will illustrate:

Holding the guide rope carefully, Pierre felt his way down the narrow rocky trail.

Before replacing the faucet, you should make sure that the water is turned off.

Tired and dusty, the hikers stumbled into the inviting shade of a large wayside elm.

To unlock the door, one should turn the key to the left.

When readers meet such opening modifiers, they tend to connect them with the nearest word possible, which is usually the subject of the sentence. Hence it is desirable, though not always imperative, that the opening modifier modify the subject. But what is most important is that the meaning be clear and that the opening be free from unintended humor. Unintentional humor, like that of the following sentence, may distract the reader's attention from what you are saying:

After being released from the men's reformatory, Professor Cahill gave Spike a job in the language laboratory.

Opening modifiers like the following are not really wrong or unclear so much as clumsy or amateurish:

In driving a heavy nail, the hammer should be held near the end of the handle.

Seeing the juicy steak sizzling over the charcoal, his mouth watered.

To catch black bass in these waters, live minnows should be used.

But a careful writer would present them in this manner:

In driving a heavy nail, you [or one] should hold the hammer near the end of the handle.

When he saw the juicy steak sizzling over the charcoal, his mouth watered.

To catch black bass in these waters, one should use live minnows.

No hard and fast rules can be given for opening modifiers except that they should be clearly related to the rest of the sentence and carefully constructed. It is best to relate them to the subject of the sentence.

REVISION PRACTICE

Retaining the same opening phrase, rewrite each sentence so that the opening phrase refers to the subject of the main clause.

1. By reading the questions carefully and thinking out the correct answers, a lot of things in the examination will be remembered for a long time.
2. When designing a jet aircraft of any type, there are many things that the engineers must take into consideration.
3. To allow plenty of room for the roots of the shrub, a deep hole should be dug by the planter.
4. While registering, my class cards got lost.
5. Speaking in this manner, the warmth and meaning of the word is lost.
6. In stating these three points, the uselessness of God has been proven by Huxley.

ADDITIONAL REVISION PRACTICE

Retaining the same opening phrase, rewrite each sentence so that the opening phrase refers to the subject of the main clause.

1. After deciding that you have enough fishing equipment, everything is loaded into the boat.
2. Stepping a little farther into the room, a bright red, foam-rubber-cushioned sofa catches your eye.
3. To make your party a success, it is necessary to have it well planned.
4. As a student, reading is the most basic skill on which my success depends.

5. After leaving high school, I think a student should work for a year before entering college.
6. At ten years of age, her parents moved to St. Louis.
7. While washing the dishes in boiling water, they are being sterilized.

15 · D
USES OF THE DASH

Among the functions of the dash, two are especially important.

1. The first important function is the use of the dash, or dashes, to set off a series as a unit from the rest of the sentence. Here are three examples, with the unit-series in the beginning, the middle, and the end positions, respectively:

Sweaters, shoes, old magazines, used scratch paper, a catcher's mitt—these had been tossed under his bed in a tangled confusion.

We have thus seen that certain qualities of character—a sense of humor, enduring patience, and a genuine fondness for young people—are necessary for success as a classroom teacher.

In addition to sports, he had numerous other strong interests—painting animals, collecting unusual rocks, cooking on the beach, and raising hamsters.

In these examples we see that in each case the unit-series is preceded or followed by a cover-all word—*these, qualities,* and *interests.*

2. A second useful function of the dash is to set off an interrupting statement or term:

My father had always insisted—and he had an insistence of iron —that one should always examine the second side of any argument.

We hiked down the coomb—known to you Americans as a gully —to search for the groundhog's den.

In typing, use two hyphens, typed together and unspaced, to represent a dash.

REVISION PRACTICE

Recopy the following sentences, using dashes where needed.

1. These three processes: leveling, sharpening, and assimilation tend to twist facts into rumors.
2. The trick knee, the mis-shapen nose, the weak ankles, all these will remain with the man throughout his life.
3. He had a new idea, it came to him in a flash, for winning the contest.
4. He was told though he did not listen that further difficulties with administrative officials were to be avoided.
5. Some men Walter Cronkite, for example, were born news commentators.

ADDITIONAL REVISION PRACTICE

Recopy the following sentences, using dashes where needed.

1. The intense struggle for power, it had now been going on for a year, was about to be resolved.
2. Several football players, Jones, Roberts, and Hanson, were about to be dropped from school.
3. It was the night of September 5 when the boy, I still cannot remember his name, finally decided the time was right.
4. The sunrise, the soft wind from the east, the smell of bacon in the air this combination, appealing to the senses, made getting up a necessity.
5. Hubert had three traits, care in research, ability to think on his feet, and skill in using language, that made him an asset to the debating team.

16 · FP
FOREIGN PLURALS

Foreign nouns are sometimes a source of confusion, both in the spelling of their plurals and in the determination of which form is singular and which is plural. See **39 Sp** for a list of foreign nouns and their plurals.

17 · Fr

FRAGMENT

A fragment is a part of a sentence written as if it were a whole sentence; that is, it begins with a capital letter and ends with a period. Usually a fragment is really a part of the sentence which precedes it. For example, "which I found in the garage" is a fragment. It sounds incomplete, as if it should be part of something else which precedes it. So let's make it a part of something which precedes it: "the purse which I found in the garage." This is still a fragment, for it still sounds incomplete. If you should say this to a friend, he would probably reply, "Well, what about the purse you found in the garage?" So let's add more again: "The purse which I found in the garage was empty." Now you have actually said something that sounds complete. It is not a fragment but a sentence.

To get the feel for completeness that is the indication of a sentence, you might try the following exercise.

EXERCISE

Here are eight pairs of word groups. In each pair one item is a fragment and the other is a sentence. Place a check before each *sentence*.

1a. Which he passed to me.
 b. I caught the ball which he passed to me.
2a. We'll leave when you are ready.
 b. When you are ready.
3a. Exhausted by the heat.
 b. The long-distance runner dropped to the ground, exhausted by the heat.
4a. Bringing supplies to the flood victims, the relief boat pulled up along the bank.
 b. Bringing supplies to the flood victims.
5a. To prepare for her mid-term exams.
 b. Helen studied diligently during the two-week vacation to prepare for her mid-term exams.

6a. By using all his skill with the paddle.
  b. Alfred managed to get through the rocky rapids by using all his skill with the paddle.
7a. The lowering sky, gray with heavy clouds and slashed with jagged streaks of lightning.
  b. The lowering sky was gray with heavy clouds and slashed with jagged streaks of lightning.
8a. My goal was to make it to the finals.
  b. My goal being to make it to the finals.

Now, see if your checks agree with the right answers, which are: 1b, 2a, 3b, 4a, 5b, 6b, 7b, and 8a. If all your answers were right, you probably are able to recognize fragments and need only to avoid carelessness in your themes to come.

If you need further help, the exercises below can aid you. In the eight-sentence exercise you just finished, each fragment had a different grammatical structure. These eight structures are now described, each followed by a short exercise. It is not necessary to learn grammatical names for these structures. The important thing is to perceive the incompleteness of the fragments and to remedy this incompleteness.

1. This kind of fragment consists of a word-group beginning with *which* or *who/whose/whom.** It is called an adjective clause. You can make a sentence out of this kind of fragment by making an addition before it, as in "I saw the candidate whom I planned to vote for."

EXERCISE (1)

Make an addition *before* each fragment, producing a sentence.

1. which was hard to handle in a strong wind.
2. who missed his morning bus to class.
3. whose bicycle was crushed by the truck.
4. which would hold ten heavy books.
5. whom I envied for his skill on the ski slopes.

* Note to instructor: *That* is omitted because it begins a restrictive clause, and restrictive clauses seldom occur as fragments.

2. This kind of fragment consists of a word-group beginning with a subordinating conjunction: *after, although, though, as, as if, as soon as, as though, because, before, if, since, unless, when, where, in case (that), in order that.* It is called an adverbial clause. You can make a sentence out of this kind of fragment by making an addition before or after it, as in "Jane decided to go, although it was raining" or "Although it was raining, Jane decided to go."

EXERCISE (2)

Make an addition *before* or *after* each fragment, producing a sentence.

1. when she returned from the class meeting
2. in order that he might toughen his muscles for the wrestling team
3. if you will lend me a necktie
4. since my brother left home
5. after the concert was over

3. This kind of fragment consists of an *-ed/-en* verb form followed by more words. It is called a past participle phrase. An example is "stunned by the upset." You can make a sentence out of this fragment in two ways: (1) Add a sentence before or after it, as "Stunned by the upset, we were silent" or "We were silent, stunned by the upset." In each of these sentences, "stunned by the upset" is a past participle phrase. (2) Use *stunned* as the main verb, as in "We were stunned by the upset."

EXERCISE (3)

For the purpose of helping you to avoid fragments in your writing, the most useful practice here is for you to add a sentence *before* each fragment, producing a longer sentence (like this: "Georgia stepped back, frightened by the spider").

1. devoured with curiosity.
2. eaten up by mosquitoes.
3. broken into many pieces.
4. built on the edge of the cliff.
5. sent by her mother.

4. This kind of fragment consists of an -*ing* verb form followed by more words. It is called a present participle phrase. An example is "singing loudly all the way." You can make a sentence out of this fragment by adding a sentence before it, making a longer sentence, as in "They marched gaily, singing loudly all the way."

EXERCISE (4)

Add a sentence *before* each fragment, making a longer sentence.

1. catching the frisbee high in the air.
2. sighing with relief.
3. waiting for the hour to end.
4. listening to the rock band on the hi-fi.
5. chewing his pizza vigorously.

5. This kind of fragment consists of *to* plus a verb, followed by more words. It is called an infinitive phrase. An example is "to lessen the cost." You can make a sentence out of this fragment by adding a sentence before it, making a longer sentence, as in "I omitted the optional equipment to lessen the cost."

EXERCISE (5)

Add a sentence *before* each fragment, making a longer sentence.

1. to choose a durable ball-point pen.
2. to send his son to college.
3. to provide a rink for ice skating.
4. to sink softly into a luxurious bed.
5. to mend the tear in her blouse.

6. This kind of fragment consists of a word-group beginning with a preposition: *at, by, for, from, in, of, on to, with, about, above, after, against, before, behind, below, because of, in spite of, by means of, owing to*. It is called a prepositional phrase. Here are two examples:

1. Ruth maintained a respectable grade-point average. In spite of the long hours she worked at the restaurant.

This should read as one sentence:

Ruth maintained a respectable grade-point average in spite of the long hours she worked at the restaurant.

2. Saul was bored with water sports. From having worked at the beach all summer as a life guard.

Here again, the preposition fragment is just a part of the preceding sentence:

Saul was bored with water sports from having worked at the beach all summer as a life guard.

EXERCISE (6)

Put each of these preposition fragments at the end of a sentence.

1. because of all the disturbance in the hall.
2. from where we sat on the sidelines.
3. against the strong pull of the current.
4. by searching through the large junk pile of spare parts.
5. owing to the distance he lived from school.

7. This kind of fragment consists of a noun with its modifiers but with no main verb. An example is:

Our campus with its green lawns, its shady trees, and low red-brick buildings grouped around a central bell tower of white marble.

To make this noun fragment a sentence, supply a main verb. Here are several ways in which this can be done:

1. Our campus with its green lawns, its shady trees, and low red-brick buildings grouped around a central bell tower of white marble **is** the pride of our community.

2. It **formed** a lovely scene, our campus with its green lawns, its shady trees, and low red-brick buildings grouped around a central bell tower of white marble.

3. Visitors **admired** our campus with its green lawns, its shady trees, and its low red-brick buildings grouped around a central bell tower of white marble.

4. Our campus **has** green lawns, shady trees, and low red-brick buildings grouped around a central bell tower of white marble.

EXERCISE (7)

Make a sentence out of each of these noun fragments:

1. the newly varnished basketball floor with spectator stands on each of its long sides

2. the old yellow school bus which made a morning rou[...] up students
3. an excellent choice for our new coach
4. the sale that the band members promoted to earn money for new uniforms
5. a suitable site for the proposed gymnasium

8. This kind of fragment consists of a noun plus an *-ing* or *-ed/-en* form of the verb, often with completing or modifying words. It is called an absolute structure. Here are three examples of the absolute-structure fragment:

1. The car lay upside down. *Its wheels still turning.*

2. They closed the meeting. *An agreement having been reached.*

3. The team returned to the dugout. *The second baseman infuriated by the umpire's call.*

These three examples can be corrected thus:

1. The car lay upside down, its wheels still turning.

2. They closed the meeting, an agreement having been reached.

3. The team returned to the dugout, the second baseman infuriated by the umpire's call.

EXERCISE (8)

Following the pattern of the examples above, put each absolute-structure fragment at the end of a sentence.

1. her heart beating violently.
2. the pain being gone.
3. the lights having been left burning.
4. his hunger extinguished by the horror.
5. her pension payments coming in regularly.

REVISION PRACTICE

Rewrite the following so as to eliminate fragments.

1. The new teacher soon became popular. By taking time to answer questions and by being free enough for students to come at any time for help.
2. My aunt moved into a new apartment. Decorated in different shades of blue with a walkout balcony and a view of the lake.

summer we had a heavy rain. Which
...se to a dangerous level.

... the wide road is hemmed in by trees on
...g the driver a feeling of security.

...given permission to use the family car. Unless the
... dangerously slippery.

AD...NAL REVISION PRACTICE

Rewrite the following so as to eliminate fragments.

1. The following day he felt even worse. Which could have been a factor in his miserable performance.
2. One can begin his task in another way. By using all his spare time to organize his material.
3. They sat on the edge of their seats. Excited by the rhythms of the two big bands.
4. Grace was happy about the personality and tact of her unseen new roommate. Who had written her three times.
5. The wrecking ball landed heavily against the wall. Which crumbled in a cloud of dust.
6. He was covered with mud from head to foot. Having practiced on a muddy field for two hours.
7. Our travel up the mountain side was slow and laborious. Our packs being loaded with heavy gear.
8. He never lost sight of his chief ambition. To understand the inner workings of the legislature.
9. The boys who decided they were no longer interested. They were the very ones who had insisted on holding the meeting in the first place.
10. We are asking you to come earlier than the previously announced time. With everything that you were requested to bring.

18·H

USES OF THE HYPHEN

The hyphen is a petty nuisance that cannot be ignored. It is useful in joining two or more words together into a cohesive, single-part-of-speech unit, like the adjectival *heavy-duty* (tire) and *devil-may-care* (attitude). In many cases, however, one is uncertain whether to use it or not. In publishers' stylebooks and in the manual of the Government Printing Office, there are multitudinous rules for hyphenating—really too many for human consumption—and these rules are not always consistent with one another. Desk dictionaries too have inconsistencies, both among themselves and within the covers of a single dictionary. For example, we find the hyphenated noun *play-off* in *Webster's New Collegiate Dictionary*, but the unhyphenated *playoff* in the *Standard College Dictionary*. Moreover, in the same *Webster's*, *money-maker* is listed as a hyphenated word, *money changer* as two words, and *moneylender* as one word. Both dictionaries are reputable, as are about four others that might be recommended by your instructor.

How then does a student know when to hyphenate? The general answer is two-part: (1) Do not try to memorize a set of rules. (2) Look up the word in question and follow the usage in your dictionary, assuming that your dictionary is approved by your instructor. If your dictionary does not have the word, then make your own choice of three forms: two words (like *fire control*); a single, unhyphenated word (like *fireman*); or a hyphenated word (like *fire-eater*).

There are, however, two individual matters that deserve note:

1. Division of words. When a word is divided at the end of a line, a hyphen is used; and rules are available for such division. However, only secretaries and printers really need to know how to divide words. For the student, the way is easy: Do not divide words at the end of the line; or, if you must divide, consult your dictionary to see where the divisions are. The dictionary uses mid-high periods within the word to show the points of division.

2. Ambiguous noun phrase. When two modifiers precede a noun, the structure may be ambiguous. Take, for example, *dirty book salesman*. We do not know whether this means a salesman of dirty books or a dirty salesman of books. A hyphen can resolve the ambiguity: *dirty-book salesman* or *dirty book-salesman*.

REVISION PRACTICE (Division of Words)

Using your desk dictionary, locate the division points in these words and put a slant line at each point. Example: en/vi/ron/ment.

accomplishment   many
efficient   enterprising
accommodate   finished
enough   reasonable
abroad   definite

REVISION PRACTICE (Ambiguous Noun Phrases)

Rewrite these sentences, using hyphens to resolve ambiguity.

1. We contributed to the Christian Children's Fund.
2. That school has a growing boy problem.
3. New student rooms are now available.
4. Did you see the nude art authority?
5. This bank deals only in large farm loans.

19 · M

MEANING NOT CLEAR

The symbol **M** indicates that you have not made your meaning clear or have stated it inaccurately. It is doubtless clear to *you,* but either you have not chosen the right words or you have not arranged them in the right way to state your meaning clearly and accurately to your reader.

Here is an example of a sentence that would be labeled with the marginal symbol **M:**

[The writer is describing the reference room of a college library.] In the center of the room is a large card file surrounded by tables covering the rest of the floor and bookshelves along the wall.

The meanings here splatter out in several directions. Yet a little more care in phrasing could have produced a clear sentence like this:

In the center of the floor is a large card file surrounded by tables, and by bookshelves along the wall.

Or like this:

In the center of the floor there is a large card file surrounded by tables, and there are bookshelves along the walls.

In the next two examples, the writer has not stated the meaning with sufficient accuracy:

> Many people have physical disabilities that they do not know about. One of the most important of these is vision.

In this passage the writer has actually said that *vision* is an important physical disability, but vision is not a disability at all. The addition of a single word can make the meaning accurate:

> Many people have physical disabilities that they do not know about. One of the most important of these is defective vision.

Here is the second example:

> The importance of good physical condition, developed by a rigorous training program, is the most basic of all football fundamentals.

In this sentence the writer has said that *importance* is a basic football fundamental. Here the elimination of three words will produce the desirable accuracy of meaning:

> Good physical condition, developed by a rigorous training program, is the most basic of all football fundamentals.

In the careful writing you are expected to do in college, it is imperative that you write clearly and accurately.

REVISION PRACTICE

Rewrite these sentences in such a way as to state clearly and accurately what you think the intended meaning of the writer was.

1. I thought eye contact and speed were among the significant weaknesses in the delivery of the speeches.
2. West Branch has a breakdown of about five religions.
3. These trees are the tallest things in the world.
4. On both sides of the hall is located an office.
5. The most important factor leading to my decision was because of the principal of the school.
6. Suicide is one of the most deadly killers.

ADDITIONAL REVISION PRACTICE

Rewrite these sentences in such a way as to state clearly and accurately what you think the intended meaning of the writer was.

1. A good example of the core program is illustrated by the high schools of Los Angeles.
2. There are also seventeen gasoline stations in the city, three of which include either a motel or a cabin court in addition to the Clark Hotel.
3. The Webster City squad suffered only two major injuries which was reflected in their brilliant season record.
4. Subject matter, organization, eye contact, and the speaking voice are factors to be developed in public speaking. Constant practice is the only way to overcome each of these points.
5. Another law frequently broken is exceeding the speed limit. The law was made because of the poor condition of many of our highways, compared to our modern high-speed automobiles.
6. Sex is the basis for life and existence. Hopefully, it will soon be offered in every school.
7. By rehabilitating a prisoner is to return him to a crime-free life in society.
8. I was walking to my art class, taking another route as usual.
9. The old and dusty marshal of Wallbrook threw the saloon door open and entered with all eyes staring.
10. The school has a good science department which consists of animals for observation and dissecting.
11. Nothing, no matter how challenging, no matter how difficult is not worth not attempting to conquer it.

20 · Mis

MISPLACED MODIFIER

A misplaced modifier is a word or word-group which has been so placed that readers are not sure what it goes with. Of course, they can usually find out by reexamining the sentence, but they should not be required to waste their time in this way. Besides, if readers are perplexed—or amused—their thoughts are diverted from what the writer has to say. A sentence with a misplaced modifier can usually be satisfactorily revised by placing the modifier in a different position, though occasionally a rearrangement of other sentence parts becomes necessary. In the example which follows, the writer says something probably not intended:

> I spent the afternoon talking about books I had read with the librarian.

A simple change in the position of the modifier will make the sentence clear:

> I spent the afternoon talking with the librarian about books I had read.

The following misplaced modifier may cause the reader to smile with amusement and forget what the writer is saying:

> He has a blue satin ribbon around his neck which is tied in a bow.

To correct this, we need only to change the position of one little word-group:

> Around his neck he has a blue satin ribbon, which is tied in a bow.

If you take pains with the arrangement of the parts of the sentence, you can avoid the embarrassment of misplaced modifiers.

REVISION PRACTICE

Rewrite these sentences, eliminating the misplaced modifiers.

1. After that, Harvey came to the band practices that I called with his horn.
2. There is also a bar located in the heart of town which is filled to capacity every evening.
3. He had an old radio that he later traded for a new television set which he loved to tinker with.
4. The senator talked about the high cost of living with several women.
5. I propose the following: Instead of a permanent marriage certificate, a temporary license would be issued to a couple that would expire in two years.

ADDITIONAL REVISION PRACTICE

Rewrite these sentences, eliminating the misplaced modifiers.

1. We have older houses for middle-income people with capacious front porches.

2. This movie portrays life as it is in a well-written plot.
3. I noticed a small window in the tunnel which was broken.
4. I have this opinion because I have seen several youths while under the influence of alcoholic beverages.
5. You will notice a small circular disk protruding from the watchcase, which is commonly referred to as the stem.
6. He had a plastic hat on his head which was on fire.
7. Rappelling is a sport that involves climbing down cliffs with ropes backwards.

21 · MM

MIXED METAPHOR

A metaphor is an implied likeness between unlike things. An example will illustrate:

> As Vicki lay in her sleeping bag, her thoughts frisbeed around a long time before she dropped off into a restless sleep.

The likeness implied here is between thoughts and frisbees. The movements of Vicki's thoughts are likened to the movements of a frisbee—slow curves, veering unexpectedly and shifting in pace and direction.

> In the opening lecture the professor spun his wheels for ten minutes before he began to move ahead.

In this metaphor the writer finds a likeness between a professor and a car in snow and uses it to picture vividly the professor's dilly-dallying before getting down to business in his lecture. Another example:

> Once on the crowded dance floor, Lou lost his rudder and began to collide with every nearby craft.

Here the likeness between Lou and a boat that can't be steered is used to reveal Lou's clumsiness on the dance floor.

Metaphors help to make your writing clear and lively and readable. But if you use two or more metaphors together, there is danger that they may clash and result in a *mixed metaphor*. Let's start with this good metaphor:

A storm of protest is blowing up.

This metaphor links the rise of protest with the growing intensity of a storm. It is a simple, everyday metaphor and expresses the idea effectively. Now, consider a different metaphor:

We must nip that protest in the bud.

Here the protest is likened to a flower. The protest must be stopped before it develops, just as a flower is prevented from developing by nipping off the young bud. Nothing wrong here. However, look what can happen when the two metaphors are brought together:

A storm of protest is blowing up, and we must nip it in the bud.

Now we have a mixed metaphor because it says that a storm, not a flower, must be nipped in the bud. The two metaphors that have been brought together here clash; they are inconsistent, incompatible.

Another example may help to clarify further:

You should not bite the hand that lays the golden egg.

Obviously, a hand does not lay an egg. The writer of this one has brought together two well-known and acceptable metaphors

You should not bite the hand that feeds you.

You should not kill the goose that lays the golden egg.

into one mixed metaphor.

The mixed metaphor is to be avoided because it calls attention to itself by its inconsistency or unintended humor and thus diverts the reader's attention from what you are saying.

Mixed metaphors are likely to occur in your first draft, when you are speeding along to set your thoughts down on paper. There are two ways to revise a mixed metaphor. Either make a plain un-metaphorical statement of what you mean, or change to a single, consistent metaphor. Here are examples of these methods of revision.

1. Mixed metaphor:

A storm of protest is blowing up, and we must nip it in the bud.

2. Revision as plain statement:

Protest is increasing, and we must stop it before it gets out of control.

3. Revisions as single, consistent metaphors:

The rumble of protest is growing louder, and we must muffle it.

The fire of protest is spreading, and we must plow up a barrier before we get burned.

A wall of protest is going up, and we must demolish it if we are to move ahead.

Protest is beginning to flood the community, and we must dam it off before it drowns us.

Sometimes you can revise a mixed metaphor by using both methods, that is, by retaining one metaphor and changing the other to plain statement. Here is an example.

1. Mixed metaphor:

The college merry-go-round of activities has always seemed so enticing that everyone is ready to jump on without weighing it in the balance.

2. Revision by single metaphor and plain statement:

The college merry-go-round of activities is so enticing that everyone is ready to jump on without thinking of the consequences.

REVISION PRACTICE

Revise each sentence by making it a plain statement or by using a single consistent metaphor or by employing both these methods.

1. To climb the ladder of success, you must leave no stone unturned.
2. I got stuck in the mud with a math problem but managed to get untangled with the aid of my roommate.
3. Unless we plow the profits back into the business, we will pump dry the goose that lays the golden egg.
4. To make homecoming a success, we must bend our shoulders to the wheel and get going under full sail.
5. If you are going to wade through freshman composition without floundering, you must really get your teeth into it.
6. As we pack up for the bus ride back to camp, I quietly chalk up another day under the belt.

7. In his reply to the question, the congressman straddled the fence with one ear to the ground.

22 · NS

NONSTANDARD

Standard English is the normal language of educated persons. It is the language in which the important affairs of the community and the country are conducted. It is the language of reputable books, newspapers, and magazines. It is the language of industry and government. It is the language of the professions—law, medicine, education, science, theology, and the like. It is the language that society expects you, as a college student, to use. You probably have a reasonably good command of it already and need only to be reminded of occasional uneducated usages that you may have acquired in your earlier life.

Nonstandard English is the language of those who have not had the advantages of education. It is the language of millions who are good people, respectable and hardworking. It exists primarily in the spoken form. It is able to do the tasks expected of it and is often vigorous and colorful. For example, "I seen you was busy" does efficiently its task of conveying information: it is clear and concise. And moreover, there is vigor and color in "I've school-taught them boys three year now, and it's beginning to taste of the keg."

Both Standard English and Nonstandard English have their own areas of usefulness, and each is inappropriate or out of place when it ventures into the territory of the other. In your college themes a usage that is marked **NS** is out of place, like track shoes on the dance floor or swimsuits in church. A **NS** usage is a matter of grammar, word choice, or idiom. Here are three examples:

1. (grammar) The letter he had *wrote* was lost.

2. (word choice) He *busted* his arm.

3. (idiom) All *to* once, the hail poured down.

Often the correction of a nonstandard form requires the change of only a single word, and your instructor may make the change instead of writing **NS**. If the instructor does so, make sure you understand the change.

REVISION PRACTICE

Rewrite, removing the nonstandard expressions.

1. Most of the freshmen girls was at the rally.
2. A gray, nondescript cat was setting quietly on the doorstep.
3. The next contestant drug his bawling calf to the arena.
4. Our carpenter refused to use them split boards.
5. Where was you when I phoned?

ADDITIONAL REVISION PRACTICE

Rewrite, removing the nonstandard expressions.

1. He couldn't hardly wedge the knife into the narrow crack.
2. In the tidal wave that followed the quake, many persons were drownded.
3. The chart was laying right in front of him.
4. George and him carried the injured man on a stretcher to the waiting ambulance.
5. Our center played very good during the last quarter.

23 · OBS

OVERBURDENED SENTENCE

An overburdened sentence is one that is too long and too heavy. Such a sentence is hard to read and should be broken up into two or more sentences. The inexperienced writer tends to continue a sentence on and on, fighting through a thicket of clauses and phrases, not knowing when or how to stop. This may be all right for the first draft, where you are getting your ideas down on paper regardless of form and style; but in the first revision you should spot all such marathon sentences and break them into shorter sentences.

Here is an example of a long-winded sentence that puts strain on the reader:

The plot includes Madame de Renal, who is married to a boring husband who thinks only of his personal prestige in society, Mademoiselle de la Mole, who is bored, rejects her boring suitors, and when she does meet an ambitious and exciting man, she remains restrained because of her noble birth and high position in society, Julien Sorel, the hero and the third son of a poor Verrières water-mill worker, who in spite of his humble birth, becomes involved with both Madame de Renal and Mademoiselle de la Mole.

Toward the end we also notice that the writer has lost control and has produced two ambiguities. Let us try to improve this sentence without altering the sense.

The plot includes a varied array of characters. Madame de Renal is married to a boring husband who thinks only of his personal prestige in society. Mademoiselle de la Mole, who is bored, rejects her boring suitors; and when she does meet an ambitious and exciting man, she remains restrained because of her noble birth and high position in society. The hero is Julien Sorel, the son of a poor Verrières water-mill worker. In spite of Julien's humble birth, he becomes involved with both Madame de Renal and Mademoiselle de la Mole.

This revision is now clear and readable. For further help in rebuilding overburdened sentences see **25 Paral, 41 Sub,** and **26 Per.**

REVISION PRACTICE

Rewrite each overburdened sentence, breaking it into two or several sentences.

1. A person in high school may be exceptionally large and go out for football not because he wants to but because if he does not he may think that people will talk about him and call him "sissy" or maybe a person is very tall and goes out for basketball not because he likes the game itself but because he is afraid of what people will say if he doesn't.
2. Another of my most powerful motives for choosing Mrs. Finney "The Best Teacher I Ever Had" was because of the understanding and ability to help someone out of a low spot which they would invariably suffer during the course of a semester, and instill instead a highly confident knowledge that sooner or later you would pull out of your more or less mental slump and fight your way through the mental blocks that now stand.
3. Professors should be very careful about grading papers where there is no set dividing line to differentiate between grades, for a paper that is poorly graded could result in the further down-

fall of the student, and a paper that is graded to the best of the professor's ability could lead to better work on his part, and though of course this does not hold true for every student, in general this is true.

4. His future was assured and he knew it, so he supported every wild plan anyone could think of, and he never worried about a thing like the rest of us who were never certain where our next meal was coming from and often didn't particularly care, although we were sensible enough to know that we had to meet at least simple needs to carry on.

5. If Tom had only known what to do and the correct time to do it, he would have been able to stay in school but he was a poor planner and a poor organizer and his failure could have been predicted, for these faults are predictors of failure in academic work and for any other kind of work for that matter.

ADDITIONAL REVISION PRACTICE

Rewrite each overburdened sentence, breaking it into two or several sentences.

1. Stevenson portrays his main character as a person who started taking the easy way out of working by stealing and shows that even though Markheim was nervous and frightened at what he did, he kept on committing crimes until he finally committed murder.

2. Finally, as I began to get all my classrooms located and bought most of the books I needed, I thought back on how much more confusing this week at college would have been had it not been for the professors and members of the university staff who took time off and went to extra trouble to help the incoming students feel at home and a little less confused in coming to such a large school.

3. Therefore, the author believes sin leads to social disorganization because Hebraism believes sin leads to complete disruption of obedience to the moral law which Hebraism believes leads to sound order.

4. Try to remember where you were last and whether or not you had the book at that time, and, if you cannot remember, try to think of someone who spent the day with you and a visit with that person may help you to recall events that will refresh your memory and give you a clue as to where the book is.

24 · ¶/no ¶

PARAGRAPH DIVISIONS

Paragraphing is a typographical convention used to aid the reader by marking the divisions of thought within an essay. Usually each division of thought introduces a new topic or a new aspect of the same topic. The topic of a paragraph is the word, phrase, or sentence by which that paragraph could be labeled or summarized.

A paragraph is often built around a topic. If a new topic is brought into the discussion, that fact may be indicated by a paragraph division, that is, an indentation. Here is an example of the end of one paragraph and the beginning of a new one from a theme on weather forecasting:

> . . . From the various cloud formations, then, a clever forecaster can arrive at a pretty fair guess about tomorrow's weather.
>
> An even better basis for forecasting, however, is the pattern of atmospheric pressures. . . .

The most frequent errors in paragraphing are these three: failing to indent, indenting too often, and introducing irrelevant material into a paragraph.

1. Failure to indent often results in a paragraph that seems to break right in the middle.

> In the history of man there have been different ideas about equality. There was absolute civil equality for the caveman. He had the same chance as his neighbor to kill a lion, or he could let the neighbor kill it and then try to kill the neighbor. The Greeks and Romans gave civil equality to those of noble birth. A patrician could be insane and have the vote, while an intelligent plebeian could not even voice an opinion. With the American Revolution, civil equality came to mean that all people were equal under the law. The idea of civil equality is still an ideal; we have far to go to make it a reality. Not everyone in our country can vote; not everyone has an equal chance for justice in the courts; not everyone has the opportunity for an education that will allow him to compete with others of equal talent; and we do not even pretend that everyone has the same social opportunities.

This paragraph develops two distinct though related topics. Thus the paragraph should be split in two:

In the history of man there have been different ideas about equality. There was absolute civil equality for the caveman. He had the same chance as his neighbor to kill a lion, or he could let the neighbor kill it and then try to kill the neighbor. The Greeks and Romans gave civil equality to those of noble birth. A patrician could be insane and have the vote, while an intelligent plebeian could not even voice an opinion. With the American Revolution, civil equality came to mean that all people were equal under the law.

The idea of civil equality is still an ideal; we have far to go to make it a reality. Not everyone in our country can vote; not everyone has an equal chance for justice in the courts; not everyone has the opportunity for an education that will allow him to compete with others of equal talent; and we do not even pretend that everyone has the same social opportunities.

2. The opposite fault, indenting too often, is perhaps more common. Beginning writers tend to paragraph every two or three sentences. Here is an example:

In preparing to read a play, one should first make a diagram of the stage and the properties it contains. This will be helpful in following the dramatic action.

Next, if any characters are described before the dialogue begins, one should make a mental picture of them. This will help to people the mind with living characters instead of puppets.

The third step is to glance quickly over the cast of characters, noting the main ones.

Now one is ready to begin the play.

All of these sentences develop a single topic, how to prepare to read a play, and should have been put into a single paragraph.

3. A third common error is introducing irrelevant material into a paragraph. All material ought to be related to the topic of the paragraph.

In terms of a statistical method or design, Gibson does not attempt any proof of his theory by testing or analysis. His article offers only speculation. There are no concrete results listed, only further speculation. *People should not be careless. Carelessness is the seed from which imperfection springs. This approach can ruin scientific research and make results almost meaningless.* Gibson feels that if his theory is correct, memory, which is the recalling of past images into consciousness, is an incidental accompaniment of learning and not its basis, as has been traditionally believed. Gibson lacks clarity. One does not write papers for learned journals carelessly defining terms and concepts. It is strange indeed that the article was even published.

For more information on the paragraph, see "Developing Thought in Paragraphs," pages 136–149.

REVISION PRACTICE

Try to make the paragraph indentions in the following passages coincide with the introduction of new topics. As you work, eliminate any irrelevant passages.

1. There were some problems during the first week of school. Getting oneself lost seemed to be the major difficulty; I think almost everyone had that problem at one time or another.

   I noticed also that many people had trouble in getting the proper books for the proper class.

   My biggest complaint was the manner in which things were done. Everywhere we hurried to get into line; then we stood and waited.

Make three paragraphs out of the following:

2. A writer should be aware of this important difference between speaking and writing: speaking is loose and writing is tight. In speaking we usually do not use orderly and carefully planned sentence structures. Instead we string together phrases and clauses as thoughts pass through our minds. These usually group themselves into sentences, it is true, but the sentences are likely to be imprecise and loose-jointed; and they often contain more words than are really needed to express our meaning. Sometimes too we become entangled in a long, intricate sentence and have to thrash our way out through a morass of mixed constructions and illogical wording. At other times we find ourselves unable to put into words exactly what we want to say, and we must resort to periphrasis and to fumbling around with words that are close but not exact. All these things are characteristic of the spoken style. It tends to be broken up and inexact and wordy, and we describe it by the word *loose*. Writing, on the other hand, is tight. It is carefully prepared, and may undergo revision after revision before taking its final form. Thus each phrase and clause can be placed in the most strategic position, and the proper adverbs and conjunctions

can be employed as connective tissue to hold the various parts together. Excess words can be pared away so that the style will be muscular rather than fatty. The most exact word can be used because the writer, unlike the speaker, has plenty of time to search for it. Written style, then, is smooth and sinewy and succinct, and we describe it by the word *tight*.

25 · Paral
PARALLEL STRUCTURE

When a number of items are presented in a series, each item should have the same grammatical form. That is to say, each item should be a noun or an adjective or a prepositional phrase or an infinitive, and so on. A passage having all members of a series in the same grammatical form is said to be parallel, or to have parallel structure. Parallel structure is desirable because it helps to make writing consistent, neat, and easy to follow. In each of the following pairs of examples, the first sentence contains a violation of parallel structure, and the second sentence maintains parallel structure. As you study them, notice how the second sentence has been made parallel and how this parallel structure increases the ease in reading.

Poor To make his organization clear, the speaker can blueprint his plan in advance, number his points, or many other things that will keep the audience on the road.

Better To make his organization clear, the speaker can *blueprint* his plan in advance, *number* his points, or *do* many other things that will keep the audience on the road. [Series of verbs]

Poor These three qualities I have discussed—a friendly attitude toward others, neatly dressed, and orderly management in the classroom—are the requisites of a good teacher.

Better These three qualities I have discussed—a friendly *attitude* toward others, neat *appearance,* and orderly *management* in the classroom—are the requisites of a good teacher. [Series of nouns]

Poor The principal of our school was required to teach subjects as well as acting as administrator.

> *Better* The principal of our school was required *to teach* subjects as well as *to act* as administrator. [Series of infinitives]

REVISION PRACTICE

Tidy up these sentences by using parallel structure where it will be helpful.

1. The job of the agency is to examine returns, investigate them when necessary, and referring the violations to the proper authorities.
2. The final step is to replace all of the chrome metal that had been taken off and removing all the masking tape.
3. The article was divided into two sections for two reasons. First, to give the reader some facts and figures on advancements in jet aviation; and second, the last section of the article was written for the purpose of informing the reader when and where the first jet aircraft was invented.
4. Some students coming to college are dependent on others to see that they get places on time, look neat, and various other things to be done.
5. The rooms will be much larger, decorations more elaborate, a tile bath, and plenty of wardrobe closets.
6. Four characteristics of a good salesman are these: neat appearance; capable of meeting the public; well informed on such subjects as world affairs, sports, and politics; and a firm believer in the product he sells.

ADDITIONAL REVISION PRACTICE

Tidy up these sentences by using parallel structure where it will be helpful.

1. It is difficult to make a decision between sitting down to study or to go to a movie.
2. The refreshments should be simple, something all can eat, and gaily decorated and appetizing.
3. The stem of a watch has two functions—that of keeping the springs taut to insure constant running and used to set the hands if the watch runs slow or fast.
4. The five steps are as follows: (1) stating the problem, (2) un-

biased observation, (3) hypothesis, (4) induction, and (5) conclusion.

5. The students learn how to take notes, read faster and understand more, ways to improve their vocabulary, and many others.

26 · Per
PERIODIC STRUCTURE

Let us look at two kinds of sentences—a firm one and a loose one. Here is an example of the first:

> In today's world, to make a good living, it is necessary that you have a marketable skill.

In this sentence we notice that, until we reach the very end, the structure is incomplete and thus the attention is held. This is called a *periodic sentence*.

The opposite of a periodic sentence is a *loose sentence*. In a loose sentence, the main part comes first, and then lesser parts—clauses, phrases, and individual words—are added. Thus the loose sentence may be stopped at one or more points before the end. Here is an example:

> You must have a marketable skill in order to make a good living in today's world.

This sentence, we notice, can be stopped after *skill* and after *living*. The loose sentence is characteristic of conversation, and in writing it produces an effect of casualness and informality.

Too many loose sentences can make your writing appear flabby and loose-jointed, whereas too many periodic sentences may make it look stiff and formal. The two types are used together in good writing. The point here is this: Do not write a loose sentence when a periodic sentence would be more effective. Let us examine a few loose sentences and note how they are tightened by revision into periodic sentences.

> *Loose* The stage looked dark and ominous at the opening of the curtain.
> *Periodic* At the opening of the curtain the stage looked dark and ominous.

Periodic The stage, at the opening of the curtain, looked dark and ominous.

Loose The college should provide better classrooms, many students believe.

Periodic The college, many students believe, should provide better classrooms.

Periodic Many students believe that the college should provide better classrooms.

Loose A bargain is sometimes a poor investment because people who put on bargain sales do not always carry quality merchandise.

Periodic Because people who put on bargain sales do not always carry quality merchandise, a bargain is sometimes a poor investment.

These illustrative sentences have been made periodic by the simple device of putting subordinate details at the beginning or in the middle.

REVISION PRACTICE

The sentences for revision that follow are not necessarily poor sentences, but you will learn a valuable lesson in emphasis by making them periodic.

1. Students in college should try to avoid too many outside activities if it is at all possible.
2. We were concerned more and more with the deficiencies of the program as time went on.
3. The world would be a much better place to live in if people would first get rid of some of their major faults which stand in their way.
4. The lecture on a sociolinguistic approach to social learning was the high point of the evening in some respects.
5. Their leader became frightened and uncertain after he thought of all the punishments he had promised to bring to bear on the guilty men.

ADDITIONAL REVISION PRACTICE

The sentences for revision that follow are not necessarily poor sentences, but you will learn a valuable lesson in emphasis by making them periodic.

1. Kurtz fell to his lowest depths through greed and through losing all contact with the civilized world, which had succeeded in keeping his baser emotions in check.
2. The loss of his billfold was the greatest tragedy, though the blowout and its ensuing delay accounted for our late arrival.
3. The intellectual must be capable of rendering sound and rational advice based on accurate reasoning, unlike the merely intelligent person who is concerned with the objective problems of life.
4. The well-trained teacher is broadly educated, has a strong liberal arts background, and has an avid interest in current affairs, according to John T. Laurence.

27 · Poss
POSSESSIVE

It is sometimes difficult to decide whether to use the *of* possessive or the *'s* possessive. With animate things, either form may be used, though the *'s* is more common:

The dog's leg

The leg of the dog

With inanimate things, however, writers of English tend to prefer the *of* possessive:

The leg of the table

The ceiling of the room

Since the possessive form of a noun is not differentiated from the plural form in speech, students sometimes forget to mark this distinction in their writing. A simple rule to follow is this. Write the word (whether singular or plural) as it is spelled without the possessive ending. If the word *as it stands* does not end in an *s* sound, add *'s*. Here are some examples:

Word As It Stands	Possessive
hero	hero's
man	man's
men	men's
lady	lady's
Harold	Harold's

But if the word *as it stands* ends in an *s* sound, add either the apostrophe alone or *'s*, depending on which sounds the more normal to your ear. These examples will illustrate:

Word As It Stands	Possessive
heroes	heroes'
France (ends in an *s* sound)	France's
Jones	Jones' Jones's
ladies	ladies'
boys	boys'

Note the difference in meaning between the singular and the plural possessive:

The boy's canoe	= the canoe of the boy
The boys' canoe	= the canoe of the boys (joint ownership)
The girl's cats	= the cats of the girl
The girls' cats	= the cats of the girls
The lady's apartment	= the apartment of the lady
The ladies' apartment	= the apartment of the ladies

A few pronouns form the possessive with *'s:*

another's, each's, each other's, either's, one's, one another's, other's, neither's
anybody's, everybody's, somebody's, nobody's
anyone's, everyone's, someone's, no one's

Observe, however, that the possessive forms of the personal pronoun do NOT take an apostrophe: *its, his, hers, ours, yours, theirs.* Examples:

Its fur is long and glossy.

Is this book his or hers?

Theirs is the white car with the blue top.

REVISION PRACTICE

Add or delete apostrophes as needed. Change the *'s* to an *of* possessive when it seems desirable.

1. Jones book had been out over a year.
2. The sale of mens and boys clothing accounted for most of their financial success.

3. Heroes awards are exciting events at the time presented.
4. To everyones disgust he had forgotten his lines.
5. I am going to analyze Huxleys and Jungs views on religion, and by this method decide which authors viewpoints I would like to add to my own.
6. The storys ending was a happy one.
7. Its bottom was covered with barnacles.

ADDITIONAL REVISION PRACTICE

Add or delete apostrophes as needed. Change the *'s* to an *of* possessive when it seems desirable.

1. The families traits were all recorded in the experiment.
2. Iris purpose in answering the letter was obvious enough.
3. The companys success was determined by its dynamic leadership.
4. The rest of the report was completed on Nicks own time.
5. The ships sinking was the years important event.
6. Some teachers ask their students to correct each others papers.

28 · P Mod
PUNCTUATION OF RESTRICTIVE AND NONRESTRICTIVE MODIFIERS OF NOUNS

Nouns are often modified by clauses and phrases. These clauses and phrases can be divided by their function into two groups, *restrictive* and *nonrestrictive*. In a given sentence, the punctuation of a clause or phrase that modifies a noun is determined by whether it is restrictive or nonrestrictive. These terms sound more forbidding than they are; we will make them clear by using examples.

We will deal with adjective clauses first and then go on to four other types of modifiers of nouns that are also punctuated according to whether they are restrictive or nonrestrictive.

An *adjective clause* is a clause which follows a noun and modifies that noun. Here are three examples:

The forward *who made the winning basket* is a sophomore.

We watched Harrington, *who is an expert microbiologist,* carefully place the specimen on the slide.

The subscriptions *that Carolyn sold during the summer* enabled her to enter junior college in the fall.

An adjective clause normally begins with *who (whose, whom), which,* or *that.* These words are called relative pronouns. When the relative pronoun is an object of a verb or of a preposition in the clause, it may be omitted, as in

The motorcycle (*that*) *I want* is a Honda.

Many students have difficulty in punctuating adjective clauses. The difficulty arises from the fact that sometimes we use commas to separate the clause from the rest of the sentence, and sometimes we use no punctuation at all. The problem is to know when to punctuate and when not to.

First, here are three rule-of-thumb tests that will tell you when NOT to punctuate:

1. If the adjective clause begins with *that,* do not punctuate.

   The tie **that** he chose was blue and gray.

2. If you can substitute *that* for *who (whom)* or *which,* do not punctuate.

   The novel **which** I like best is Richard Wright's *Native Son.*

3. If the *whom, which,* or *that* may be omitted, do not punctuate.

   The dormitory (**which**) he lives in is Baker Hall.

   The club was highly pleased with the president (**whom**) they elected.

The best way to approach the problem of punctuating adjective clauses is to examine their meaning and function. For example:

College students **who show initiative and responsibility** should be advanced rapidly.

Here the *who* clause restricts *college students* to certain ones only. Thus this is a *restrictive clause.* A restrictive clause is not set off by commas.

College students, **who need relaxation as much as anybody,** should engage in social activities at frequent intervals.

In this sentence the reference is to ALL college students; there is no restriction. The *who* clause merely adds a descriptive detail. A *who* clause like this one, descriptive only, not restricted, is a *nonrestrictive clause*. A nonrestrictive clause is set off by commas. Now let us try two more:

> The team **which wins the tournament** will be given a party by the losers.

Here the *which* clause points out which particular team out of all teams will be given a party. It restricts the party receiver to one certain team. Here again we have a restrictive clause, and no commas are used.

> The Happy Hoboes softball team, **which has won 12 out of 13 games,** is given the best chance to win the tournament.

In this sentence there is no restriction by the *which* clause. This clause simply adds further information; hence commas are used. It may be useful to remember that after any proper name, the *who* or *which* clause is nonrestrictive and commas are used.

The following sentences are correctly punctuated. If you understand why, you should be in the clear.

> The city that was damaged most by the flood was Omaha.

> St. Paul, which is a manufacturing city, is the capital of Minnesota.

> Those students who have not taken their health check must report to the Health Center.

> We entered the Auditorium Building, which was being repaired, and tried to find the registrar's office.

> Mary Moran, who lives in the next corridor, goes home nearly every weekend.

> The girl whom I take to the formal must be a good dancer.

REVISION PRACTICE

The sentences below all contain adjective clauses beginning with *who (whom)*, *which,* or *that.* They are all unpunctuated. Apply the tests that have been discussed above and put in the commas that are needed.

1. Everyone was there except Harry who knew the purpose of the meeting was hopeless.

2. Ticket orders which are not accompanied by checks will be ignored.
3. He who wants the most from his college education must develop regular study habits.
4. They will have little good to say of any person who is selfish and inconsiderate.
5. Although it was an unusually warm day Avis who was wearing a heavy woolen sweater appeared cool and poised.
6. The belief that the pain will subside in a few hours is absolutely unfounded.

ADDITIONAL REVISION PRACTICE

Punctuate the following sentences, applying the principles discussed above.

1. Henry Cutler who has not missed a meeting in three years should certainly be a member of the committee.
2. These are the trails which have been designated for beginners.
3. Her broker who was supposed to be an expert cost her dearly within a month's time.
4. They were hunting the Mandarin goose which is found in Asia.
5. People who had long considered the move were at this point holding back.
6. The next shock that I received was when I discovered the great amount of material available.
7. She bought the television set which had the truest color.

The restrictive-nonrestrictive distinction is also true of other modifiers that follow a noun. Here are four cases:

1. A phrase beginning with an *-ing* verb:

Restrictive The man *shouting at the players* is the line coach.
Nonrestrictive There stood George, *shouting at his sister to be careful.*

2. A phrase beginning with an *-ed/-en* verb:

Restrictive The car *driven by his 15-year-old son* had a crumpled fender.
Nonrestrictive That shiny black car, *driven only to a few funerals,* would be a good buy.

3. A noun meaning the same as its preceding noun:

Restrictive	His cousin *Sally* brought the picnic basket.
Nonrestrictive	Sally, *his cousin,* brought the picnic basket.

4. A prepositional phrase:

Restrictive	The barn *at the head of the valley* belongs to our neighbor.
Nonrestrictive	King Charles' castle, *on the top of a steep cliff,* looks down over the valley.

With all these structures, commas are used in the same way as with modifying adjective clauses. If the modifier limits, if it points out which specific one, then no commas are used. For example, in the four sentences labeled "restrictive" above, the modifiers point out which man, which car, which cousin, and which barn. Therefore these modifiers are restrictive, and no commas are needed. But in the four "nonrestrictive" sentences the modifiers do not point out; they just add a descriptive detail or further information, and so they are nonrestrictive and require commas.

REVISION PRACTICE

Applying the principles discussed above, insert commas in the following sentences to set off the nonrestrictive modifiers. Do not use any commas for the restrictive (point-out) modifiers. They are all unpunctuated.

1. The grass *on the south side* was getting dry.
2. Our new brown baby poodle *frightened by the explosion* cowered under the table.
3. We were shouting for Rapid Fire *the horse with the white mane* to win.
4. The next batter *swinging his bat* slowly walked up to home plate.
5. The girl *sitting on George's left* is an East Indian but the one on his right is an American.

29 · Quot
MECHANICS OF QUOTATION

1. Quotation marks are used primarily to mark words represented as actually spoken or written:

He said, "It is unwise to consider any promotion at this time."

The promise in your letter was to "love, honor, and obey."

Notice that the quotation is marked whether it is a complete sentence or just part of a sentence; quotation marks indicate that the enclosed words are those of the speaker or source, and not your own.

2. An *indirect quotation* differs in that the material quoted is not necessarily in the exact words of the speaker; therefore, it does not require quotation marks:

He said that her dress was becoming.
    (His exact words were: "Your dress is becoming.")

Jenkins remarked that it would be better to wait.
    (His exact words were: "It is better to wait.")

She said she didn't care.
    (Her exact words were: "I don't care.")

Jenkins remarked that it is better to wait.
    (His exact words were the same in this case: "It is better to wait.")

3. A *quote within a quote* is marked by single quotation marks:

She asked, "What is this 'science of the mind' to which the author refers?"

4. You should also refresh your memory on a few special uses of quotation marks and italics.

4a. Underline the titles of books and the names of newspapers, periodicals, plays, movies, operas, and musicals. Underlining in writing or typing is the same as italics in printed matter.

4b. Place quotation marks around the title of a work represented as a part of a book, such as the title of a story, poem, article, section, essay, or chapter:

The material for this essay was found in "The Age of Absolutism," a chapter in Burns' <u>Western Civilization.</u>

4c. Underline any word that is referred to as a word, as in

The word <u>pi</u> is used by printers.

4d. Use quotation marks to enclose a slang term in a formal context, as in

He was arrested for having "grass" in his possession.

4e. Use quotation marks to enclose a word used in a special way, as in

We called him "doc" because he was expert in first aid.

5. A bothersome question related to the use of quotation marks is this: "Shall I put the punctuation inside or outside the quotes?" You will usually be able to handle this question if you remember these three rules:

5a. The comma and period are *always* placed *inside* final or closing quotation marks.

"Sing it brightly," he said.

He said, "Sing it brightly."

The conclusion of the essay is marked by the word "therefore."

5b. It is always correct to place the semicolon and colon *outside* quotation marks.

"Let your conscience be your guide"; with this remark he left the room.

"Think big": this is the motto of the advertising world.

5c. The question mark, exclamation mark, and dash are placed *inside* or *outside* the end quotation marks, depending upon whether they punctuate the quoted words only or the entire sentence.

"How old is your sister?" he asked.

"Stop that noise!" she shouted.

Is this the answer I get, "No one is at home to you"?

What a stirring command, "Trust thyself"!

"The quality of mercy"—and by this Portia means human mercy—"is not strained."

6. Let us examine one last problem. You have already noticed that a short quotation (less than three lines) is simply incorporated in the body of the text; it may be introduced by a comma, dash, or colon, or it may appear as an independent sentence:

We often find it best, in a discussion of literature, to begin with Aristotle's definition: "Tragedy, then, is an imitation of an action."

or

We often find it best, in a discussion of literature, to begin with Aristotle's definition. "Tragedy, then, is an imitation of an action. . . ."

Long quotations (more than three lines) are separated from the main body of the text by spacing and by indentation. They do not need quotation marks because the spacing and indentation serve to set off the quotation from the rest of the text, as in this example:

Hazlitt spoke of a natural euthanasia many years ago when he stated:

We do not in the regular course of nature die all at once: we have mouldered away gradually long before: faculty after faculty, attachment after attachment, we are torn from ourselves piecemeal while living. . . . The revulsion is not so great, and a quiet euthanasia is a winding-up of the plot. . . .

Three periods used here (. . .) indicate that words have been omitted at that point. The fourth period marks the end of a sentence. This is a convenient device for cutting out irrelevant material in quotations, so long as you do not disturb the structure or meaning of the sentence.

REVISION PRACTICE

Supply the punctuation that is missing.

1. He said, I'll not bring up the matter again. This is final.
2. He said that he wouldn't bring up the matter again.
3. The contract reads but the buyer is responsible for all repairs.
4. Jack remarked I definitely heard you say She is not at home.
5. Our textbook, Pre-Columbian Art, has a chapter entitled The Sculpture of the Olmecs.
6. Did you enjoy the movie Moonstone
7. Professor Haskins reads the New York Times every Sunday.
8. Her favorite poem was Stopping by Woods.
9. I don't understand the word charisma.
10. We always referred to Harry as the top banana.

11. Where are you going he asked
12. Were you there when he said This party stinks

ADDITIONAL REVISION PRACTICE

Supply the punctuation that is missing.

1. Come over to my place he said and let's talk it over.
2. To thine own self be true these words of Polonius are memorable.
3. He shouted angrily Get out of here
4. Why do you think he said We'll put it off till next week
5. Never have I heard such an unnerving comment as You'll find out soon enough
6. How brazen of him to say I knew you'd come across
7. The word with has two meanings that are the opposite of each other.
8. Jaspers was reading an article, Masters of Babble, in Harper's.
9. Whatsoever thy hand findeth to do, do it with thy might these words of Solomon rang through his mind.
10. The words of the registrar boomed through the auditorium. Registration is the process of signing up for classes. New students receive advice from faculty members in planning their schedules, and all students fill out cards and material for the use of various offices on campus. The last step in registration is payment of bills, and the student is not registered until financial arrangements have been completed. Information about courses and fees is contained in a publication with the title, The Academic Bulletin. Students may pick up their registration materials Monday morning.

30 · Red
REDUNDANCY

Redundancy refers to a needless duplication of meaning; for no good reason, the same idea is repeated in different words. Redundancy frequently takes such forms as *visible to the eye, round in shape, basic fundamentals*. Thus, redundancy always leads to wordiness (see **44 W**). Both result from carelessness and haste and should receive particular attention during the revision process. Let us reduce these sentences to their essentials:

> *Poor*   She had the radio on so low it was not audible to the ear.
> *Better*   She had the radio on so low it was not audible.

> *Poor*   Eighteenth-century England was ruled by a monarchy type of government.
> *Better*   Eighteenth-century England was ruled by a monarch.

REVISION PRACTICE

Rewrite, removing the redundancies.

1. The house is low and rectangular in shape with a sloping, green roof.
2. He may notice that the sky is a bluish gray in color.
3. This program gives a person a period in which to adjust to the new surroundings that encircle him.
4. Things will be easier in future days to come.
5. The area used to be covered by water in the past.
6. Many current programs of today are topheavy with administrators.
7. The judge gave him three life sentences to be served concurrently.

ADDITIONAL REVISION PRACTICE

Rewrite, removing the redundancies.

1. In conclusion, let me close with this word of advice—cool it!
2. We have created antibiotics to rid ourselves of germs already in us.
3. You'll notice that the rose is a dusty pink in color.
4. Graves of dead war veterans were decorated with flowers.
5. In my opinion, I think there is good in both.
6. People dress more casually in today's modern world.
7. Both Lowman and Dubois are completely destroyed in the end.
8. Machines often allow people to idle away time which is carelessly wasted.

31 · Ref
REFERENCE OF PRONOUNS

The pronouns most likely to cause trouble are these: *it, they, this, who,* and *which.* In using such pronouns, writers should keep two points in mind. First, they should make sure that singular pronouns refer to singular words and that plural pronouns refer to plural words. This seems simple, yet students often write sentences like these:

> Whenever a *student* needed advice, *they* could feel free to go to Mr. Maire.

> As long as the public wants better *motion pictures*, the motion picture industry will supply *it*.

Second, the writer should make sure that the reader knows exactly what the pronouns refer to. Let us examine a few illustrative sentences from student writing:

> Men like Brodie and Kolmer discovered vaccines and gave them to the public, but *they* were not successful. . . .

Here the reader cannot tell whether *they* refers to *vaccines* or to *Brodie* and *Kolmer.* The difficulty can be easily remedied by deleting *they* and inserting words that say exactly what the writer means:

> Men like Brodie and Kolmer discovered vaccines and gave them to the public, but these vaccines were not successful. . . .

> or

> Men like Brodie and Kolmer discovered vaccines and gave them to the public, but these men were not successful. . . .

The pronouns *which* and *this* can be a special source of confusion because they may refer to a whole preceding idea or to a particular noun. In the next sentence the reference of *which* is not immediately clear:

> Each room has two study desks with only one study lamp, *which* is very inconvenient because of the poor lighting on one of the desks.

To revise this unclear reference of *which,* the writer has only to substitute a word or more which says exactly what is meant:

> Each room has two study desks with only one study lamp. This situation is very inconvenient because of the poor lighting on one of the desks.

REVISION PRACTICE

Rewrite these sentences, removing any weaknesses in the reference of pronouns.

1. Sometimes a student causes trouble simply because they have not learned what is right and what is wrong.
2. Television programs are interrupted every now and then for commercials. Some of them are very irritating.
3. After her sophomore year she began taking an athletic trainer's course. This is a person who takes care of injured players.
4. When Columbus heard that Bobadilla had in his possession a letter from the sovereigns giving him the power he was exercising, he meekly went to confer with Bobadilla.
5. He was always bringing into our room some strange dog he had found, which was a nuisance when I was trying to study.
6. These services are very worthwhile for it enables the student to actually take part in the worship.
7. Fraternity houses on the university campus would provide not only more room, but also guidance, social functions, and the development of leadership for its members.
8. The dormitory rooms have built-in closets that have eight drawers and two shelves. They have a place to hang clothes and a sliding-door cabinet to place boxes and suitcases in.
9. The rooms are heated by a radiator that is run by steam. They can be easily regulated by the student for the temperature desired.
10. A college student should know how to type by the time they enter college.

ADDITIONAL REVISION PRACTICE

Rewrite these sentences, removing any weaknesses in the reference of pronouns.

1. Kindergarten is the child's first experience at school, and they are very excited about learning.
2. Each member of the faculty had at least one school activity which they were to sponsor.
3. Many things are needed to be a good wrestler. First, they must have a knowledge of the various holds and escapes.
4. Band means a lot to a person and certainly does help them.
5. This teacher was mathematically inclined but was unable to get it across to us students.
6. The Roman farmer's occupation was closely related to his religion. They would pray to the various gods for help.
7. Since planes are not as simple as cars, one must have greater skill to fly it.
8. Giuseppe came late in a battered old car, which irritated me.

32 · Rep
REPETITION

The symbol **Rep** indicates that a word has been repeated unnecessarily and thus draws unwarranted attention to itself. This is a matter of style rather than of clarity. Note the following sentence:

Spring is the time of the year I like most, for in *spring* we hunt in the woods for *spring* flowers.

These three occurrences of *spring* make our ears ring. This excessive repetition can easily be avoided by substituting *then* for *in spring* and perhaps *the first* for the last *spring*.

Repetition in itself is not a writing fault. It is very useful in achieving coherence, as you will learn in "Achieving Sentence Flow" (pages 125–136). It is also a device for emphasis, as the following sentences show:

I *hated* the work, I *hated* the hours, I *hated* the job.

Our subject will be *patriotism:* not the cheap *patriotism* of the stump politician, but the *patriotism* of the conscientious citizen.

A simple way to discover unnecessary repetition is to read your written material aloud. To eliminate the repetition, replace the repeated word with a synonym or pronoun, or omit it altogether.

REVISION PRACTICE

Revise these sentences so as to avoid the unnecessary repetition of words.

1. He thought that this class thought it had no responsibility to uphold tradition.
2. I cannot explain what it is that makes me feel like a new man. It could be this feeling of self-confidence in my ability to be able to work hard for a good average that makes me feel that my prospects are good.
3. He did not list the important steps in order of their priority in his list of ideas.
4. The pond on the campus adds much beauty to the campus.
5. He had to report for duty at least three weeks before anyone else had to report.

ADDITIONAL REVISION PRACTICE

Revise these sentences so as to avoid the unnecessary repetition of words.

1. Because of their reaction, I felt all along that they felt this way about including Jim in the party.
2. He believed that many people believed the same story he did.
3. The furnishings with which the house was furnished were in excellent taste.
4. All these points would seem to directly point to the matter at hand.
5. I feel that new students' week was invaluable to those who took advantage of all the advantages given them.

33 · RO
RUN-ON (FUSED) SENTENCE

A *run-on sentence* (or *fused sentence*) is one that follows a preceding sentence as if both were one. There is no period and no capital letter to show the break between them (see **9 CF**). Some run-on sentences do not interfere with meaning, but they suggest that the writer is illiterate.

> Our lounge is the Rose Lounge it is very beautiful.

Others, however, leave the reader in doubt about the intended meaning:

> Of course we had to go shopping the very first day we discovered more of the virtues of this lovely city.

The preceding example might be read as one sentence, but what the writer meant was:

> Of course we had to go shopping. The very first day we discovered more of the virtues of this lovely city.

For further help with this problem, see **34 S Col** and **41 Sub.**

REVISION PRACTICE

Revise these passages so as to eliminate run-on sentences.

1. As you are completely new in this business, you are allowed certain mistakes too many, however, might cost you your job.
2. A person's character is acquired from his environment he is not born with it.
3. No single text was assigned the students found explanations in different books without exception these books supplied different answers.
4. Scholarship is recognized at this university through the dean's honor designations, scholarships, awards, and prizes a person with good grades is rewarded.
5. Was this the only solution to the dilemma it seems so.
6. Rowles is married to the former Virginia Davis they have three children.

ADDITIONAL REVISION PRACTICE

Revise these passages so as to eliminate run-on sentences.

1. She is entitled to think whatever she likes about my paper her arguments would have been more convincing if she had read it however.
2. I fervently hope you will make your voices heard beyond that I dare expect no more.

3. Think what you like I don't care.

4. Desmond misunderstands the character of the mistaken U.S. intelligence estimates with which the book is mainly concerned he engages in a useless and pointless battle with a straw man.

5. While hopes for diplomacy are being dashed, the arms race has mounted the long-range outlook is less than hopeful.

6. It was an idea not too difficult to put into practice on that basis it was quickly accepted.

7. Was all this hard work and studying of rudiments worth it I think so.

34 · S Col
USES OF THE SEMICOLON

A writer should be familiar with the three basic uses of the semicolon.

1. The semicolon is used between independent or main clauses to indicate a separation stronger than that given by a comma but less strong than a period stop.

   Harris was always generous with his children; in this respect, he was like his father.

   The comma indicates a slight pause; the semicolon is used for a stronger one.

2. The semicolon is used between independent (= main) clauses when the second clause has a transition word at or near its beginning. Some of the common transition words are *accordingly, also, besides, consequently, finally, furthermore, hence, however, indeed, instead, likewise, moreover, nevertheless, otherwise, still, then, therefore, thus.* The use of a comma or commas to set off these transition words is optional. If you want to indicate a pause to your reader, use a comma or commas, as in these sentences:

   For two hours no car had stopped to pick me up; moreover, it was beginning to rain.

   The doctor's report was not encouraging; we felt, however, that the laboratory tests might alleviate our anxiety.

But if you want an uninterrupted flow at the point of the transition word, omit the comma or commas, as in the following sentences:

We finished adding the figures; then we counted the money.

He had asked several times; hence he felt it unnecessary to repeat his request.

The dean thought our plan was impracticable; he was nevertheless willing to give it a trial.

3. The semicolon is used to separate clauses or phrases in series when commas are used within these clauses or phrases.

Replenishing the stock of the wholesale house required particular attention in the purchasing of these items on specific days: apples, oranges, and bananas on Monday; beets, radishes, and celery on Tuesday; milk, wine, and soda pop on Friday.

Experienced writers frequently use the semicolon as a strengthened comma to emphasize a pause.

The community needs a strong man; that is, one with special qualifications.

The nose may be shut off from the mouth by lifting the soft palate; or, if the soft palate is allowed to hang down freely, these make a combined resonance chamber.

REVISION PRACTICE

Punctuate the following sentences, using semicolons and commas as suggested above.

1. It is impossible to clarify the issue at this time, however, in a month or two much of the research will be in and facts not known at this time will be readily available.
2. When we are under stress we do not write as well, thus we have a harder time with an in-class theme.
3. The catalog had made it quite clear in order for a person to graduate he must have at least 128 semester hours.
4. The long grass, the broken windows, and unpainted exterior all suggested a house with no occupants, therefore it seemed surprising to observe smoke coming from the chimney.
5. The plane was to be several hours late, he knew therefore that the flat tire was not going to create an emergency.

6. Hardly anyone knew how the rumors had started, the whole town was nonetheless aware of them.

7. The following people have consented to furnish letters of reference: Mr. James C. Connor, manager of Pen Department, Chandlers Inc., Evanston, Mr. Henry Trauscht, owner, Evanston Auto Parts and Supply Co., Evanston, Mr. Josef Szmzayk, superintendent of mails, Evanston Post Office, Evanston.

ADDITIONAL REVISION PRACTICE

Punctuate the following sentences, using semicolons and commas as suggested above.

1. He had turned in his records over a month ago hence he felt no obligation to write a letter of explanation for any delay.

2. Other books by Hardy are listed for you with the dates of publication: *Far from the Madding Crowd,* 1874, *The Return of the Native,* 1878, *The Mayor of Casterbridge,* 1886.

3. His real interest lay in his business, he devoted as much time as he could however to the study of history.

4. After cutting the wood for the fireplace, he was exhausted and decided to take a nap, consequently he didn't hear the telephone.

5. I checked the directory faithfully to find the Anderson Company, which was to do the plumbing, Clifton, who was to do the wiring, Bottleson, who was the recommended cabinet-maker, and Graber, who was the interior decorator.

35 · SB
SENTENCE BEGINNING

The symbol **SB** means that you should begin your sentence in a different way. Your instructor may recommend a way by using a number after **SB. SB9**, for example, would mean the ninth sentence beginning—the infinitive—among the twelve kinds listed below.

There are at least a dozen grammatical ways to begin a sentence. If you have an active command of these twelve, it will be easier for you to start a sentence and to find ways of connecting it in thought with the preceding sentence. The most frequently used ways are these four:

1. The subject—

   Jim was *afraid of the impending examination.*

2. The adverb—

   Unfortunately, *Jim has not kept up with his assignments.*

3. The prepositional phrase—

   Before the impending examination, *Jim realized that he had neglected his work.*

4. The adverbial clause—*

   Because he had been negligent of his assignments, *Jim was fearful of the impending examination.*

The remaining kinds of sentence beginnings are more characteristic of writing than of speech, and you will find it worthwhile to master them. This is easy to do, and it will pay handsome dividends in increasing your writing skill.

5. The direct object—

   His daily assignments *Jim had neglected for several weeks.*

6. The adjective—

   Fearful of the impending examination, *Jim began to study in earnest.*

7. The present participle (-*ing* form of verb)—

   Worrying about the impending examination, *Jim stayed up all night to study.*

8. The past participle (-*ed*/-*en* form of verb, like *praised, beaten*)—

   Deprived of study time by play practice, *Jim found himself unprepared for the impending examination.*

9. The infinitive (*to* + a verb)—

   To keep up his grade average, *Jim kept faithfully to his study schedule.*

* An adverbial clause is a word-group that begins with words like *if, as, unless, though, because, as soon as, since, when.*

10. The absolute construction—*

Examination time approaching, *Jim set aside an hour a day for review.*

11. The coordinating conjunction (*and, but, for, or*)—

Jim wanted to participate in the Homecoming festivities and try out for the leading role in the first play of the drama workshop. But examination time was near.

12. The appositive before the subject—

A playboy during the semester, *Jim now had to face the ordeal of final examinations.*

REVISION PRACTICE

Revise the following sentences, using the sentence beginnings suggested in the parentheses.

1. Frank made several hurried changes in plans in order to meet Ginger at the hour they had set. (Infinitive)
2. Bill Pace was a contender for class honors. Yesterday he failed the mid-term examination. (Appositive)
3. He was relieved of his duties and left his position under a cloud of suspicion. (Past participle)
4. Hoping for an agreement on a rate increase, the board of directors called an early meeting. (Subject)
5. The old plane, which was slow and noisy, was used for short runs and for emergencies. The new one was used for daily passenger service. (Coordinating conjunction for second sentence)
6. He uttered an enthusiastic exclamation and left the room. (Present participle)
7. His difficulties were resolved during the coming months. (Prepositional phrase)
8. The committee had not planned the program of the annual art festival early enough to get the services of well-known speakers. (Direct object)
9. John had probably insisted on an early payment. (Adverb)

---

* The absolute construction is a sentence-part not grammatically connected with any other part of the sentence. Examples: (1) *The church being closed,* Hawkins knocked on the door of the rectory. (2) *A cigar in his mouth,* Sweeney studied the cards.

10. Harry was indignant about the noise in the library and wrote a letter of complaint to the *University Daily*. (Adjective)

11. Barry had the driver in his hand and stood watching the young couple trying to get off the first tee. (Absolute construction)

12. New members had to be appointed, for the safety committee had been negligent in its duties. (Adverbial clause)

36 · SV
SENTENCE VARIETY

A series of sentences following the same pattern tends to become monotonous. The passages below exemplify this problem. Each is followed by an improved passage showing an acceptable solution.

Subject-verb pattern
The team quickly lined up for the next play. The quarterback crouched low. He barked out the signals. The ball was snapped to him. He wheeled to the right and feinted a pass. Then he plunged straight through center. He slipped at the line of play and could not regain his feet. So he was downed without a gain.

Improved
Quickly the team lined up for the next play. Crouching low, the quarterback barked out the signals. When the ball was snapped to him, he wheeled suddenly to the right, feinted a pass, and plunged straight through center, but slipped just at the line of play. Unable to regain his feet, he was downed without a gain.

Present participle beginning
Having heard a scratching noise at the lake shore, Pete stumbled out of the tent and peered through the darkness. Having bought a brand-new canoe, he was worried about someone's stealing it. Seizing his flashlight, he ran down the path toward the boathouse. Turning the light on the canoe, he saw a fat coon scuttle away.

Improved
Having heard a scratching noise at the lake shore, Pete stumbled out of the tent and peered through the darkness. Because his canoe was brand-new, he was worried about someone's stealing

it. He seized his flashlight and ran down the path toward the boat-house. As he turned the light on the canoe, he saw a fat coon scuttle away.

REVISION PRACTICE

Rewrite each passage to eliminate the monotony of grammatical pattern.

1. *Present participle beginning:*
   Having finished his class work for the following day and having no exciting plans for the rest of the evening, Frank decided to stay home. Browsing through his limited library, he found nothing at all he had not already read. Yawning and groaning at the same time, he decided to go to bed.

2. *Passive voice pattern:*
   The course is intended to introduce freshmen in the humanities course to Italian art. The history of art forms is studied from the Early Renaissance through the Baroque Period. Styles of painting and sculpture are analyzed. The gradual development of realism is examined. The principal works of major artists are used as illustrations by the instructor.

3. *Adverbial clause beginning:*
   Since Norma was late this morning, she found herself running toward the bus stop. When she turned the corner, she saw her bus pulling away from the curb. After she had waved frantically at the departing bus and had lost her breath chasing it, she sat down on the curb and burst into tears.

37 · So P
SHIFT OF PERSON

The word *person* is here a grammatical term that can best be understood through examples. The personal pronouns are classified into three persons—first, second, third—according to their role in the speaking situation. The pronouns in the first person refer to and include the speaker, for example, *I* and *we*. The pronouns in the second person refer to the one or ones spoken to, for example, *you*.

The pronouns in the third person refer to the one or ones spoken of, for example, *he* and *them*. The third person also includes all nouns. Here is a table showing the words that belong in each of the three person-classes:

Person	Singular	Plural
1st	I, my, mine, me, myself	we, our, ours, us, ourselves
2nd	you, your, yours, yourself	you, your, yours, yourselves
3rd	he, his, him, himself	they, their, theirs, them, themselves
	she, her, hers, herself	
	it, its, itself	
	All other pronouns, for example, everybody, everyone, one's, other, this, that	ones, others, these, those
	All nouns, for example, student, person, teacher	

The writer must be consistent in using grammatical person and not shift aimlessly from one person to a different person. The most common mistake with grammatical person is to shift without cause to *you* in the middle of a passage that is written from the first-person point of view (*I* or *we*) or the third-person point of view. Here is an example of this common mistake:

> It is hard for me to write because I can never think of the right words that will best express what you are trying to put down on paper.

It is obvious that the *you are* should have been *I am*. This was a shift from the first to the second person. In the next example the shift is from the third to the second person:

> Meeting new people broadens a *person's* train of thought and develops *your* personality.

This might have been written in either of two ways. If the writer had been addressing the reader directly in the paper, using the second person *you,* then the sentence might have been written:

> Meeting new people broadens *your* train of thought and develops *your* personality.

If, on the contrary, the writer had been using the third person, then this person should have been kept throughout:

Meeting new people broadens a *person's* train of thought and develops *his* personality.

REVISION PRACTICE

Revise these sentences so as to eliminate inconsistent uses of grammatical person.

1. In high school I liked grammar because it was easy for me, and you could grasp it on your own.
2. When we had received our bedding, we were shown how to make one's bed according to army regulations.
3. When a person enrolls for a two-year course, he must follow a prescribed schedule set up by the college. The reason for this is that you will get the classes that will be most helpful to you as a teacher.
4. I need to understand what good writing is. To be able to express yourself in writing is of great importance.
5. College, to me, marks the beginning of a new life, a demanding life, from which you can expect to receive only as much as you give.
6. I liked this course better than my first year's work. You were on your own in using the library and finding references.

ADDITIONAL REVISION PRACTICE

Revise these sentences so as to eliminate inconsistent uses of grammatical person.

1. Many of these writings I thoroughly enjoyed, and they offered an extra advantage in that they taught one to read properly.
2. I wanted to find out all the rules I needed to know to keep you out of trouble.
3. By the end of one's first year, you feel you know just about all the answers.
4. He believes that all man needs to do is to get all the facts and you will get the correct answer.
5. I like being out on the prairie where you can look for a mile in any direction.

38 · SI
SLANG

Slang terms are often vivid and colorful and sometimes seem to express exactly what you have to say; and their proper place is in informal and intimate writing addressed to readers for whom slang is a common medium of expression. However, in the formal or semi-formal style expected in much college writing, they should be used sparingly if at all. There is nearly always an equivalent for a slang term in the standard vocabulary. Consider, for example, "He goofed in the last examination." For *goof* there is a wide array of substitutes, most of which you know: *blunder, bungle, err, flounder, botch, mismanage, fail.*

Slang cannot be defined with precision, but we can make a few descriptive statements that will help to identify slang words:

1. Slang is lively and picturesque.
2. It is usually short-lived, being here today and gone tomorrow.
3. It varies with different speech communities. High school slang differs from college slang, and British slang from that in the United States.
4. It is found more in speech than in writing.
5. It is made up of certain kinds of words:
   a. Clipped words—*prof, deli, vibes.*
   b. Newly invented words—*pizzaz, nerd, icky.*
   c. Words borrowed from jargon, that is, from the specialized vocabulary of a profession, trade, or similar restricted group—"Let's go to your *pad.*"
   d. Old words with new meaning—"He was *stoned,*" "Don't be *chicken,*" "He got busted for possessing *grass.*"
   e. Standard words used figuratively—"They had a *blast* last night."

You may be tempted to ask, "Really, what's wrong with slang?" This is a fair question and merits an answer. First, slang terms tend to lose their liveliness through overuse, like an old tennis ball. They become worn-out vouchers for imprecise thoughts and usurp the place of more fitting and vigorous words. Second, many slang terms belong to an in-group and are not understood by outsiders. Thus

their use with outsiders is a form of social rudeness. In a college
theme, if you must use a slang expression to convey your thought,
remember to put it in quotation marks.

39 · Sp
SPELLING

The symbol **Sp** represents one of two writing faults:

1. An actual misspelling, like *proceedure* for *procedure*.
2. A choice of the wrong word, as "We may *loose* the game," instead of *lose*.

If your fault is an actual misspelling, you may find the word on
the list in the inside back cover, which consists of words that college
students frequently misspell. If it is not there, you will have to look
it up in your desk dictionary.

If the **Sp** represents a wrong-word choice, you are likely to find
your incorrectly used word in **45 WW,** together with the word you
should have used.

Words Often Misspelled

See the list, inside back cover.

Spelling of Foreign Plurals

Different languages have different ways of signaling plurality in
nouns. When foreign nouns are borrowed into English, some retain
the spelling of their foreign plurals, as in *data,* the Latin plural of
datum. Others will in time take on the English *-s/-es* plural in addition to the original plural, giving us two plural forms, as in *cur-
ricula* and *curriculums.* Still others will adopt the English plural
and lose their foreign plural, like *sonatas.* Your dictionary will give
you the plural form of every noun that has a plural other than the
normal *-s/-es* form.

Here is a short reference list of the more frequently used nouns
that have a foreign plural. In scientific writing the foreign plural
is often preferred when there is a choice.

Singular	Plural	Singular	Plural
addendum	addenda	memorandum	memoranda
			memorandums
alumna	alumnae	millennium	millennia
alumnus	alumni		millenniums
analysis	analyses	neurosis	neuroses
apparatus	apparatus	opus	opera
	apparatuses		opuses
appendix	appendices	parenthesis	parentheses
	appendixes	phenomenon	phenomena
basis	bases		phenomenons
concerto	concerti	radius	radii
	concertos		radiuses
crisis	crises	species	species
criterion	criteria	stadium	stadia
curriculum	curricula	stimulus	stadiums
	curriculums	stratum	stimuli
datum	data		strata
diagnosis	diagnoses	syllabus	syllabi
erratum	errata		syllabuses
formula	formulae		
	formulas	synopsis	synopses
focus	foci	thesis	theses
	focuses	virtuoso	virtuosi
hypothesis	hypotheses		virtuosos
medium	media		
	mediums		

40 · Sbj
SUBJUNCTIVE

In written English and in careful spoken English, special forms of the verb, labeled *subjunctive,* are employed in three sentence-situations:

1. The form *were* is used instead of *was* or *is* in contrary-to-fact word groups beginning with *if, as if,* and *as though.*

   If I *were* a doctor, I'd prescribe rest for you.

This *if* word group is contrary to the fact or reality because the speaker, I, is obviously not a doctor. Hence the verb form *were.*

He acts *as if* he *were* the owner.

Here *were* is used because the word group "as if he were the owner" is contrary to the fact or reality that he is not the owner.

The wind blew *as though* a hurricane *were* approaching.

Again, *were* is used because "as though a hurricane were approaching" is contrary to the truth that a hurricane is not approaching.

2. When the verb *wish* is followed by a word group, the verb form *were* is used instead of *was*.

   I *wish* I *were* there.

Here we note that the group "I were there" is contrary to the fact or reality, namely, that the speaker is not there at all.

3. In some word groups that follow a verb or an adjective and begin with *that*, the dictionary-entry form of the verb, such as *go, be, revise,* is used instead of the *-s* verb form, such as *goes, is, revises*.

   It is *necessary that* she *go* to the meeting.

   The regulations *require that* we *be* on stage early.

   The teacher *insisted that* Harold *revise* his paper.

The verbs that require this subjunctive form are non-action verbs like *ask, demand, suggest, order, prefer, advise, provide, desire*.

The subjunctive forms above occur in writing and careful speech. In casual speech, other forms and structures are often used, as in

If I was a doctor, I'd prescribe rest for you.

He acts as if he's the owner.

I wish I was there.

It is necessary for her to go to the meeting.

REVISION PRACTICE

Underline the form in parentheses used in writing and careful speech.

1. If she (were was) home, she'd answer the phone.
2. He plays as if he (was were) determined to win the match.
3. Jane wished she (were was) at the beach.

4. The dean asked that I (am be) at his office at three.
5. It is advisable that he (hires hire) a tutor for math.

ADDITIONAL REVISION PRACTICE

Underline the form in parentheses used in writing and careful speech.

1. If that lawyer (was were) skilful, he could win the case.
2. George wishes he (was were) well enough to being jogging again.
3. Her mother preferred that Isabelle (choose chooses) the career of a dental assistant.
4. Jack limps as though his ankle (was were) strained.
5. If that (were was) the case, he should apologize.

41 · Sub
SUBORDINATION

The symbol **Sub** indicates that you should change an independent clause into a subordinate element. To begin, let us take the sentence

George felt exhausted after the long exam, and he decided to relax at a light movie.

and subordinate the first part, using each of four kinds of subordinating elements.

1. A clause beginning with a word like *after, although, as, because, before, if, since, unless, when, while:*

Since he felt exhausted after the long exam, George decided to relax at a light movie.

2. An adjective clause beginning with *who, whom, whose, which,* or *that:*

George, who felt exhausted after the long exam, decided to relax at a light movie.

3. A phrase beginning with an *-ing* verb:

Feeling exhausted after the long exam, George decided to relax at a light movie.

4. A phrase beginning with an *-ed/-en* verb or an adjective:

Exhausted after the long exam, George decided to relax at a light movie.

Weary after the long exam, George decided to relax at a light movie.

Subordination is a matter of writing style about which there are no absolute rights and wrongs. The general principle is this: Put the important part of your message in an independent clause and the supporting or collateral parts in subordinate elements.

REVISION PRACTICE

The sentences in the following revision exercises are not necessarily poor ones, but by revising them you will gain skill in manipulating subordinate elements. Use the suggestions in parentheses.

1. Most people are afraid of their first driver's examination, and they are unable to take it with any degree of confidence. (Begin with the adjective *afraid*.)
2. Monsieur Vaillot was a lawyer, and he knew exactly what to say to the other driver. (Do this two ways, using *because* and *who*.)
3. You must report regularly and on time or your entire career may be in jeopardy. (Use *unless*.)
4. We filled our glasses and then drank a toast to absent friends. (Use *after*.)
5. The half-time show was much too long, so the opening of the second half had to be delayed ten minutes. (Do this in two ways, using *since* and an *-ing* verb.)

ADDITIONAL REVISION PRACTICE

Revise the following sentences, using the suggestions in parentheses.

1. Her dress for the prom was not ready, so Jane had to wear an old blue one. (Subordinate with *as*.)
2. I had a plan in mind. It was to jog a half mile every day after my three o'clock class. (Begin with *The plan which*.)
3. The article was clear and readable, and the author used ter-

minology that even the layman could understand. (Subordinate with *because*.)

4. I finally located the proper street and then headed for the nearest pub. (Begin with an *-ing* verb.)

5. In the front lounge Laureen met Scott, and he promptly complimented her on the color scheme of her attire. (Subordinate with *who*.)

42 · TS
TENSE SHIFT

You must be careful in your use of the tense forms of verbs to show time. When you do not select the tense form which would indicate the precise time relationship that you have in mind or when you shift from one tense to another without reason, you may confuse your reader or muddle the time perspective in your writing.

1. One problem occurs in writing about events of the past:

> It *was* Jefferson's belief that the safety and the freedom of the colonies *is endangered* by England.

> Sandra *is offered* her first job in the second chapter. Three chapters later she *accepted* it.

You may present such events either in past or present tense (the latter is called *historical present*), but you must choose one tense or the other and stick with it.

> It was Jefferson's belief that the safety and freedom of the colonies *were endangered* by England.

> Sandra *is offered* her first job in the second chapter. Three chapters later she *accepts* it.

or

> Sandra *was offered* her first job in the second chapter. Three chapters later she *accepted* it.

2. It is also easy to misuse tenses in indirect quotations. For example, in using Samuel Pepys' statement, "This play is the most licentious to come on the stage all year," a student may carelessly write:

Samuel Pepys *said* that this play *is* the most licentious to come on the stage all year.

A safe rule to follow in such situations is this: Use the past tense in the indirect quotation when the main verb of the sentence is in the past tense.

Samuel Pepys *said* that this play *was* the most licentious to come on the stage all year.

Use the present tense, however, when the meaning of the quotation is true in the present.

Francis Bacon sincerely *believed* that reading *makes* a full man.

REVISION PRACTICE

Revise the following sentences, paying particular attention to the tenses of the verbs.

1. While you were looking the other way, a miracle happens. Without even noticing, you made the green light at Third Street.
2. Just when he thought the work was finished, he finds another problem to do.
3. She seemed utterly uninterested in the contest when suddenly she jumps up and screams, "Sock 'em!"
4. The church believes that we will never lose our moral standards because so long as we believed in a God, we can regard Him as the source of our moral ideas.
5. At the end of her story she got her facts all mixed up; she is sure, however, that no one doubts the truth of her tale.

ADDITIONAL REVISION PRACTICE

Revise the following sentences, paying particular attention to the tenses of the verbs.

1. Jeanne allowed Fred to spend all his money on her; leaving him after it is gone is selfish on her part.
2. The author calls for a religion that makes life simple, clean, and beautiful and gives a high standard to men. He wanted a religion like this because he wanted to think of himself as being highly intelligent.

3. Then I ask if she wants to go out with me, but she brushed me off with a look and left me standing there.

4. Finally, as I got all my clothes situated and bought my books, I think how confusing this week at college would have been.

5. Thus we can see that religion has evolved or at least seemed to have evolved.

43 · Tr
TRANSITION

Sentences should flow smoothly, one into the other. One way to achieve this flow of thought is to make sure that the first part of a sentence refers back to the preceding sentence. (Other ways are discussed in "Achieving Sentence Flow," pages 125–136). When there is a gap in thought between two sentences, your instructor may use the symbol **Tr**. This indicates that you need some word or word-group to bridge the gap.

1. Sometimes all you need to do is add a transitional word or phrase such as *next, besides, then, however, thus, consequently, furthermore, indeed, in addition, therefore, moreover, hence, nevertheless, on the contrary, as a result.* This passage will illustrate:

> My adviser was the first person I consulted. He suggested that I drop one course. I went to see the dean, who willingly consented to the change.

Here the addition of a single word will effect a smooth transition:

> My adviser was the first person I consulted. He suggested that I drop one course. Then I went to see the dean, who willingly consented to the change.

2. At other times, you may need to revise the second sentence so that the first part of it refers back to the previous sentence. Here is an example:

> Harris tore a ligament in his shoulder at the first tennis match. He was unable to play for a month after that.

In this case a change in the position of one phrase will make the transition:

Harris tore a ligament in his shoulder at the first tennis match. After that he was unable to play for a month.

In the next example the second sentence must be readjusted and a clause inserted to make the transition:

Johnson worked day and night to get his report ready before the deadline. The president praised him for his conscientious effort when the report was finished and turned in.

Here it is again, with the first sentence flowing into the second:

Johnson worked day and night to get his report ready before the deadline. When the report was finished and turned in, the president praised him for his conscientious work.

REVISION PRACTICE

Rewrite each second sentence so as to make a transition between the two sentences.

1. After five miles of steady marching with heavy backpacks, the climbers halted in the shade of a large rock. They rested for fifteen minutes there.
2. My roommate's car broke down just as he was returning to the campus on Sunday evening. He was late to his morning class because of this.
3. During the first two weeks each student delivers four five-minute talks. An introduction of himself constitutes the first of these.
4. In the nineteenth century writers tended to write long, complicated sentences. They ordinarily used much more punctuation than is common today, in order to guide the reader through the intricate patterns of these long sentences.
5. My roommate spent most of his evenings at a nearby tavern. His semester grades were low as a result.

ADDITIONAL REVISION PRACTICE

Rewrite each second sentence so as to make a transition between the two sentences.

1. Only three members of the combo showed up to play. We decided to go on with the dance nevertheless.

2. My term paper was three weeks late. I was penalized with a lower grade for this offense.
3. Jim dubbed his first shot off the tee. He could not do anything right after that.
4. The defeat crushed us. We had one consolation, however.
5. The class meeting went on and on with unrelieved monotony. The chairman ordered a coffee break and relief came at last.
6. The chairman insisted that the motion was out of order. I could not agree with this.

44 · W
WORDINESS

Writing should be direct and spare, free from unnecessary words that serve no purpose. When you convey your thoughts with an overabundance of words, your style seems bloated and your reader is likely to become impatient. A first draft is often wordy, but when you revise you can pare away the unneeded expressions and try to achieve an economy of style consistent with accuracy of statement. Notice how a little delicate surgery improves the following sentences.

Wordy In many schools they have regular film operators.
Better Many schools have regular film operators.

Wordy I could also make some improvements in my articulation of words.
Better I could also improve my articulation.

Wordy I slur over words for the simple reason that I have become lazy.
Better I slur over words because I have become lazy.

Wordy I think my speech would have been better if I would have gotten rid of three weaknesses. The three weaknesses I have are the tempo in which I speak, the articulation of my speech, and the spurtiness of my speech.
Better I think my speech would have been better had I got rid of three weaknesses: my fast tempo, slovenly articulation, and spurtiness.

For additional exercises, see **23 OBS** and **30 Red.**

REVISION PRACTICE

Rewrite these sentences so as to express the same meaning but eliminate wordiness.

1. If you want to find the latest styles, you have to go to another town that is larger.
2. In order to achieve good grades in school, some people have to cheat for them.
3. As far as extracurricular activities go, there is a wide variety of intramural and intercollegiate sports available.
4. The other rate that is bad for the speaker is the rate that makes the speech too slow.
5. College offers many new opportunities for students, such as the following: there are countless activities that students can engage in, and there is knowledge that the students can gain from their classes.
6. Dennison has many changes that should be made in order to be a better town.
7. Without these qualities, those who study to be teachers will be nothing but failures, as far as teaching goes.
8. Both sorts of booby traps are triggered by a trap wire across the jungle path and are extremely fatal.
9. Since the cars we use today must travel at safe speeds, it takes a lot more time to go somewhere on our roads than if we could travel at a much faster speed.

ADDITIONAL REVISION PRACTICE

Rewrite these sentences so as to express the same meaning but eliminate wordiness.

1. People who have had little or no experience in the field of athletics often think that it takes only brawn and few brains to make a football player.
2. She did not realize the fact that a student studies best when he is fresh.
3. One thing that I can say is that I never attended as many dances as I did in that week.
4. In conclusion, generally then, Thoreau's essay, I believe, was written to tell the people how to remove themselves from the power of the government for their own betterment.

5. I intend to discuss the male students in this college. This group of almost five hundred men is composed of freshmen, sophomores, juniors, and seniors. They tend to fall into two main classifications: the studious students and the nonstudious students.

6. Each student has his own preference as to how he should divide his time between scholastic and social activities.

7. I would like to point out a case where the views of the church and the views of science are similar. The case in point is original sin.

45 · WW
WRONG WORD

We sometimes confuse words because of their similarity in spelling or pronunciation or meaning. The following checklist gives pairs or groups of words that students quite often use in the wrong way. (Words which are pronounced the same but which differ in spelling and meaning are called *homonyms*.)

accept Will you *accept* the offer?
except Put all *except* the spoiled ones into the basket.

advice Give me some *advice*.
advise I'll be glad to *advise* you.

affect Will it *affect* my grades. (= influence)
effect The *effect* of the collision was slight. (= result)
effect I want to *effect* a change in her behavior. (= bring about)

allusion The minister made an *allusion* to the prodigal son. (= reference)
illusion You have the *illusion* that this job is simple. (= false impression)

already They have *already* come.
all ready The performers are *all ready*.

all right Are you feeling *all right?*
a lot (This is two words.)

among A goat was running *among* the sheep.
between Tim sat *between* his father and his mother.
You must distinguish *between* juncos, vireos, and warblers.*

amount They bought a large *amount* of silk.
number They bought a large *number* of paintings. (*Number* refers to countable things; *amount,* to uncountable things.)

ascent The *ascent* to the top was steep.
assent I cannot *assent* to your demand.

beside She stood *beside* her fiancé.
besides *Besides* regular meals, they serve sandwiches.

buy Will you *buy* a ticket?
by He passed *by*.
bye Good*bye* now.

capital His *capital* is too small to open a store. (= money and possessions of value)
Begin a sentence with a *capital* letter.
The *capital* of Minnesota is St. Paul.
capitol The *capitol* is a dignified building.

censor The warden *censored* the mail.
censure The defendant was *censured* by the judge. (= reprimand, blame)

choose Be sure to *choose* the best.
chose Yesterday she *chose* a dress.

cite He *cited* the new regulation.
site The pizza shop moved to a new *site*.
sight The sun lit valley was a beautiful *sight*.

clothes *Clothes* make the man.
cloths She covered the bread with *cloths*.

complement The tie should *complement* the shirt. (= to complete, make perfect, fill a lack)
compliment Do not forget to *compliment* your hostess.

---

* Abundant evidence supports the fact that *between* may denote a distinction between *several* things or persons considered individually.

contemptible A cruel man is *contemptible*.
contemptuous A *contemptuous* remark is one expressing contempt.

continual There are *continual* interruptions. (= repeated often)
continuous The *continuous* stretch of forest was visible as far as the horizon. (= extended without interruption)

council The *council* will meet at three today.
counsel She received wise *counsel* from her adviser.

course His math *course* was difficult.
    The plane had to change *course*.
coarse This corn is ground very *coarse*.

desert Cactus grows in the *desert*.
    He received his just *desert*. (= what he deserved)
dessert Ice cream is a popular *dessert*.

credible Your story is hardly *credible*. (= believable)
credulous *Credulous* persons believe anything they hear.

disinterested The judge is a *disinterested* listener. (= impartial, not prejudiced)
uninterested Jim was *uninterested* in the lecture.

emigrate They *emigrated* from Ireland.
immigrate They *immigrated* to Australia.

eminent Dr. Mayo was an *eminent* physician. (= outstanding, renowned)
imminent A thunderstorm was *imminent*. (= threatening, dangerously near)

fewer He is smoking *fewer* cigars. (*Fewer* refers to number.)
less He is drinking *less* beer. (*Less* refers to quantity.)

finally They *finally* arrived. (= at last)
finely It was a *finely* ground powder.

forty (Note the spelling of these numbers.)
four
fourteen

formerly McCarthy was *formerly* my friend.
formally I've seen you around but we've never met *formally*.

granite The headstone was made of *granite*.
granted We cannot take her permission for *granted*.

human Gossipping is a *human* weakness.
humane To overlook mistakes is a *humane* act. (= kind)

imply The instructor *implied* that I was lazy. (= suggest, express indirectly)
infer I *inferred* from her tone that she was irritated. (= conclude)

ingenuous You can trust an *ingenuous* girl like Jeanne. (= frank, open, without guile)
ingenious George is an *ingenious* man around the house. (= inventive)

irrelevant Your remark is *irrelevant* to the discussion. (= inapplicable, not relating to)
irreverent That was an *irreverent* gesture. (= not respectful)

it's It's a nice day. (= it is.)
    It's lost a good deal of fur. (= It has.)
its Its head is small.

later We'll see you *later*.
latter The first one is too heavy; I'll take the *latter*. (= second or last)

leave We shall *leave* early.
let *Let* me help you. (= allow)

lie Why don't you just *lie* down?
lay *Lay* it on the shelf, please. (= put or place)

lying Your scarf is *lying* in the drawer.
laying They are now *laying* the foundation.

lay Yesterday he *lay* in bed all day. (= past tense of lie)
laid I *laid* the hammer on the bench. (= past tense of *lay*; = placed)

lose Don't *lose* your gloves.
loose This wheel is *loose*.

luxuriant The foilage is *luxuriant* here. (= lush and rich)
luxurious This is a *luxurious* apartment.

marital They live in *marital* harmony. (= pertaining to marriage)
martial *Martial* music arouses the spirits. (= pertaining to war)

moral Such deception is not *moral*.
morale The ski club has a high *morale*. (= spirit, esprit de corps)

oral Fred gave an *oral* report. (= spoken)
verbal We shall be studying *verbal* communication. (= communication by means of words, as opposed to gestures and physical movement)

passed He *passed* the test.
past The *past* few days have been busy.

personal This is *personal* business.
personnel Many *personnel* were injured.

precede Tuesday *precedes* Wednesday.
proceed The marching band will *proceed* to the gym.

principal The *principal* was in his office.
　　　　　Their *principal* food was rice.
　　　　　The *principal* was $25,000.
principle Honesty is a good *principle*.

quiet It was *quiet* in the house.
quite It was *quite* dark outside.
quit He *quit* his job.

raise Please *raise* the window.
rise Prices will *rise* again.

respectively The three boys were nine, ten, and twelve years old, *respectively*.
respectfully Sally spoke *respectfully* to the doctor.

role Sam will play the *role* of Macbeth.
roll He called the *roll*.

set Will you *set* the plant in the window?
sit Will you *sit* in this chair?

stationary This is a *stationary* table. (= not movable)
stationery Eleanor wrote on green *stationery*.

than Eric is heavier *than* I am.
then *Then* he left the room.

their *Their* house is white.
there We found them *there*.
　　　　There is a boat at the dock.
they're *They're* both my friends.

though *Though* the rain has stopped, you'd better take an umbrella.
thorough Merle did a *thorough* job with the housecleaning.
through She walked quietly *through* the crowd.

to She went *to* college.
too I want some *too*. (= also)
     You are *too* late. (= excessively)
two Some families have *two* cars.

weather The *weather* is sunny.
whether She doesn't know *whether* to stay or go.

who's *Who's* going to the dance?
whose *Whose* motorcycle is this?

your Did *your* mother come?
you're *You're* just in time for lunch.

Occasionally you may be trapped into using the wrong word by some resemblance between two or three words in spelling or sound or meaning. For example, the resemblance between *refute* and *repute* led a student to write this sentence:

Only by knowing Communism can we *repute* it.

And the loose links of meaning between *distinguish, differentiate,* and *decipher* lured another unwary student to pen this statement:

Every individual, no matter what his belief may be, can *decipher* between right and wrong.

If your are uncertain of a word, look it up in your desk dictionary. If this doesn't solve your problem, there is another dictionary that is exceptionally good for common words that are often confused. It is *The Advanced Learner's Dictionary of Current English* by A. S. Hornby and others. Its definitions are simple, and usually words are not only defined but put into phrases and sentences to show you how to use them. Your college library probably has it in the dictionary section.

EXERCISE

Underline the correct word in parentheses in the following sentences.

1. (It's its) fur was light gray.

2. (Their they're) trying to find (there their) shoes in the locker-room pile.
3. The (principal principle) speaker was Dr. Harrison.
4. There are (fewer less) students in college this year.
5. Isaac was (setting sitting) on the floor.
6. Before he would (except accept) my work, I had to get an excuse from my doctor.
7. I could not run for Dorm (Counsel Council) because of my grades.
8. Since Charles has been transferred to the missile (cite site) he is able to take courses at Community College.
9. My brother never liked Frank, but I find him simple and (ingenious ingenuous).
10. I found I could study for longer periods if I got up and began work at five A.M. (than then) if I began at ten P.M.
11. It was an (affect effect) with their stage lights that they had never achieved before.
12. The (preceding proceeding) class had been dull.
13. The (principal principle) conferred with the boy's parents about his grades.
14. Our class has been studying the (principals principles) of logic.
15. My roommate is (continuously continually) complaining about the food.

ADDITIONAL EXERCISE

Underline the correct word in parentheses in the following sentences.

1. The dean seemed to (infer imply) that I should spend less time on volleyball and more time on study.
2. In the first stanza the poet makes an (illusion allusion) to the myth of Philomela.
3. (It's its) necessary to eat well-balanced meals.
4. We saw (fewer less) pheasants in the cornfields this fall.
5. Won't you (sit set) down and rest?
6. My adviser's (council counsel) was to resign from the band.
7. While he said nothing, I (implied inferred) from his manner that he was angry with me.

8. Since I began keeping a regular study schedule I have had (less fewer) poor grades.

9. The motor wouldn't start, and cleaning the spark plugs had no (affect effect) on it.

10. The room was so (quite quiet) that you could hear the slightest whisper.

11. She found her notebook (lying laying) on the lab bench.

12. From (it's its) edge we peered down into the canyon.

13. The change in classes did not (effect affect) her word load.

14. At the close of opening night the (moral morale) of the play cast was high.

15. (Their there) is a spot on your blouse.

REVISION PRACTICE

Correct the wrong words in the following sentences.

1. Before he would except my work, I had to get an excuse from my doctor.

2. I could not run for the Dorm Counsel because of my grades.

3. Since Charles has been transferred to the missile cite, he is able to take courses at Community College.

4. My brother never liked Frank, but I find him simple and ingenious.

5. I found I could study for longer periods of time if I got up and began at five A.M. than if I began at ten P.M.

6. It was an affect with their lights which they had tried for weeks to achieve.

7. The principle actor was ill.

8. My roommate is continuously complaining about the food.

9. In the first stanza the poet makes an illusion to the myth of Philomela.

10. The dean seemed to infer that I should spend less time acting in the experimental theater and more time on study.

ADDITIONAL REVISION PRACTICE

Correct the wrong words in the following sentences.

1. My adviser counciled me to drop my math course and resign from the band.

2. While he said nothing, I implied from his manner that he was angry with me.

3. Since I began keeping a regular study schedule, I have had less failing grades.

4. The motor wouldn't start, and cleaning the spark plugs had no affect on it.

5. The room was so quiet that you could hear the slightest whisper.

6. She found her notebook laying on the lab bench.

7. From it's edge we peered down into the canyon.

8. The change in classes did not effect her work load.

9. At the close of the opening night, the moral of the play cast was low.

10. Charlotte took pains not to loose her umbrella.

3 MASTERING LARGER WRITING PROBLEMS

1
ACHIEVING SENTENCE FLOW

If your writing is to be clear and readable, it must have a quality that we call sentence flow. This means that each part should flow easily into the next, without gaps and without jerkiness in the forward movement of your thought. The reader should know at every point exactly where he is in relation to what has gone before. To achieve smooth sentence flow, you will find four tools of style especially useful. They are not difficult to master, and once you have learned to use them, they will do wonders in improving the readability of your writing style. These four tools are: (1) transitional devices; (2) key terms; (3) hook-and-eye links; (4) parallel repeats.

1. Transitional devices were referred to previously (see **43 Tr**). They are words and phrases that are really not integral to the sentence, but that serve to show readers a relationship that you wish to call to their attention. For example, the relationship of continuation is shown by terms such as *besides, furthermore, in addition, moreover, next,* and *to continue.* The relationship of contrast is shown by such terms as *however, nevertheless, on the contrary, on the other hand,* and *yet.* The relationship of result is indicated by such expressions as *as a result, consequently, hence, in conclusion, so, then, therefore, thus.* They are usually placed at or near the beginning of a sentence to show the relationship of this sentence to what has gone before.

OBSERVATION EXERCISE

Underline the transitional devices used in the following passages and indicate the relationships they show, that is, continuation, contrast, or result.

1. Learning to understand and use a foreign language need not be a difficult task. Moreover, in learning a new language, you will also discover a new world of manners and customs and attitudes.
2. Until three decades ago, it was generally believed that there was no authentic Chinese history before the Chou dynasty, which began about 1100 B.C. Within our lifetime, however,

knowledge has been so increased that we can push back the frontier of Chinese history 500 years.

3. In the Archaic Period the Greeks, believing in goodness, created sculpture that was otherworldly and unrealistic; yet, because they believed in reason, their sculpture became steadily more realistic.

4. Every name that one applies to someone is merely a label that refers to one aspect of the person's whole nature. For example, you can call the same person a singer, an athlete, a black, a lawyer, a churchgoer. Yet none of these refers to the whole person. However, there is usually one name (or label or symbol) that stands out in one's consciousness above the others, though the particular name that stands out will be different in the minds of different people. Thus the name or label we use to designate any given person distracts our attention from the concrete reality.

5. We cannot fully believe what we see, because we cannot trust our sense organs. Another person with his own eyes may see the same things we are looking at as being of a different color or shape. Besides, since his past experiences with things are different from ours, these past experiences will affect the way he perceives.

2. Key terms are the important basic words that are central to what you are writing. These help you in your sentence flow when you deliberately repeat them. You may have been told in your past schooling that you should strive for variety in your word choice and should avoid repeating the same word. This advice holds true for some kinds of literary writing, but not for lucid exposition, with which we are concerned. When you are writing exposition, you must keep your meaning completely clear at all points as you advance the movement of your thought; and to keep your meaning clear, you should continue to use the same word when you refer to the same thing. For example, if you are writing about how to construct a rabbit pen, you should call it a *pen* throughout your paper and not shift to synonyms like *cage* or *hutch*. Such shifts tend to confuse the reader.

Here is an example of a careful repetition of key terms. Note how easily you can follow what this student is saying:

The tempo of my speech was a little fast. If I learn to slow down when I get nervous, I will have a better *speaking rate*. If my *speaking rate* is better, then my *articulation* will improve. And when I get rid of my *articulation* difficulties, people will be interested in what I have to say.

OBSERVATION EXERCISE

In the following passage the author is talking about the meaning of words. His key terms are *word* and *meaning*. Notice that he does not find it desirable to shift from *meaning* to *sense* or *signification*, nor from *word* to *term* or *expression* or *utterance*. Instead of scattering synonyms about, he repeats and repeats his key terms, thus clearing the path of thought from unnecessary obstructions. Count the repetitions of *word* and *meaning*. (Italics for these words are supplied.)

The first thing to realize is that most of the useful *words* in our language have many *meanings*. That is partly why they are so useful: they do more than double duty. Think of all the things we mean by the *word* "foot" on different occasions: one of the lower extremities of the human body, a measure of verse, the ground about a tree, twelve inches, the floor in front of the stairs, paying the bill. Yet these are pretty distinct *meanings*—they don't easily get confused with one another. It is much more difficult to distinguish clearly among the different *meanings* that the *word* "equality" takes on when we are talking about equality before the law, equality of opportunity, equality of political rights, equality of aptitude, and so forth.

We can think of various *meanings* of some *words*, but we don't realize just how flexible language is until we look up some of the most changeable *words* in a large dictionary. *Webster's New International Dictionary*, for example, distinguishes twenty-four *meanings* of the *word* "free." . . . The editors of *The American College Dictionary* . . . found 55 distinct *meanings* of the *word* "point," in 1,100 occurrences of the *word*, and distinguished 109 different *meanings* of the *word* "run."

Monroe C. Beardsley, *Thinking Straight*

3. **Hook-and-eye links** are used when you refer in the beginning of one sentence to the end of the preceding sentence, to something near the end, or even to the preceding sentence as a whole. By so doing, you hook the two sentences together in an easy, comprehensible flow of thought. Here are two examples of hook-and-eye links:

He could hardly wait to get *under the shower. There* a gushing downburst of hot, soothing water would relax his aching muscles and tired mind.

Jim formed the habit of *reviewing his eight o'clock assignment during the quarter hour just before he went to bed.* By this means he could face his first morning class with the comfortable feeling that he had the assigned reading clearly in mind.

Especially useful as hook-and-eye links are the demonstratives *this, these, that, those,* and *such.* Of these five, the word *this* is the most frequently used. Here it is, linking the second sentence to the first:

Day after day, Harris practiced his backhand drive against the concrete wall. *This* produced a powerful stroke that helped him make the tennis team.

But *this* is also a treacherous word, as the next pair of sentences shows:

My midterm grades were dangerously low, and my counselor advised me to spend less time on social activities. *This* made me determine to budget my time.

Here the word *this* may point back to either the first or the second part of the preceding sentence. The solution of this difficulty is simple. All you have to do is to insert a word or two after *this* specifying what *this* points back to. Our illustrative sentence would have been clear if the student had written it in either of these ways:

My midterm grades were dangerously low, and my counselor advised me to spend less time on social activities. *This advice* made me determine to budget my time.

My midterm grades were dangerously low, and my counselor advised me to spend less time on social activities. *This low standing* made me determine to budget my time.

4. **Parallel repeats** are repetitions of a grammatical pattern (see 25 Paral). Such repetitions may occur within a single sentence, in a series of sentences, and even in a sequence of paragraphs. The next two examples illustrate parallel repeats within sentences:

Vigorous writing is concise. *A sentence* should contain *no unnecessary* words, *a paragraph no unnecessary sentences,* for the same reason that *a drawing* should have *no unnecessary* lines and *a machine no unnecessary* parts. This requires *not that* the writer make all his sentences short, *or that* he avoid all detail and treat his subjects only in outline, *but that* every word tell.

William Strunk, Jr., and E. B. White, *Elements of Style*

Thought marches; and marches to the rhythm of subject and predicate. *The foot that is planted on the ground represents the subject,* and
*the foot that is moving forward in the air is the predicate. All the sta-
bility is in the subject, all the movement in the predicate.*

> P. B. Ballard, *Thought and Language*

The next two examples show parallel repeats within sentences
and in successive sentences, creating a smooth flow of thought:

One day somebody should remind us that, even though there may be
political and ideological differences between us, *the Vietnamese are our
brothers, the Russians are our brothers, the Chinese are our brothers;*
and one day we've got to sit down together at the table of brotherhood.
But *in Christ there is neither* Jew *nor* Gentile. *In Christ there is neither*
male *nor* female. *In Christ there is neither* Communist *nor* capitalist. *In
Christ,* somehow, *there is neither* bound *nor* free. We are all one in
Christ Jesus. And when we truly believe in the sacredness of human
personality, *we won't* exploit people, *we won't* trample over people with
the iron feet of oppression, *we won't* kill anybody.

> Martin Luther King, Jr., "A Christmas Sermon on Peace,"
> in *The Trumpet of Conscience*

For instance, *let a person, whose* experience has hitherto been con-
fined to the more calm and unpretending scenery of these islands,
whether here or in England, go for the first time into parts where physical nature puts on her wilder and more awful forms, *whether* at home
or abroad, as into mountainous districts; or *let one, who* has ever lived
in a quiet village, *go* for the first time to a great metropolis,—then I
suppose he will have a sensation which perhaps he never had before. *He
has* a feeling not in addition or increase of former feelings, but of something different in its nature. *He will* perhaps be borne forward, and
find for a time that he has lost his bearings. *He has* made a certain
progress, and *he has* a consciousness of mental enlargement; *he does* not
stand where he did, *he has* a new centre, and a range of thoughts to
which he was before a stranger.

> John Henry Newman, *The Idea of a University*

In the following example parallel repeats assist in linking sentences
together:

If we wish to play an effective part as members of a community, we
must avoid two opposed dangers. *On the one hand there is the danger of
rushing* into action without thinking about what we are doing. *On the
other hand there is the danger of indulging* in an academic detachment
from life. This is the peculiar temptation of those who are prone to see
both sides of a question and are content to enjoy an argument for its
own sake. But thinking is primarily for the sake of action. *No one can*

avoid the responsibility of acting in accordance with his mode of think-ing. *No one can act* wisely who has never felt the need to pause to think about how he is going to act and why he decides to act as he does.

                    L. Susan Stebbing, *Thinking to Some Purpose*

The next selection shows us how parallel repeats are used to help link a sequence of paragraphs together:

The politicians tell us, "you must educate the masses because they are going to be masters." *The clergy join in* the cry for education, for they affirm that the people are drifting away from the church and chapel into the broadest infidelity. *The manufacturers and the capitalists swell the chorus lustily.* They declare that ignorance makes bad workmen. . . . *And a few voices are lifted up* in favor of the doctrine that the masses should be educated because they are men and women with unlimited capacities for being, doing, and suffering, and that it is as true now, as ever it was, that the people perish for lack of knowledge.

These members of the minority, with whom I confess I have a good deal of sympathy, *question* if it be wise to tell people that you will do for them, out of the fear of their power, what you have left undone, so long as your only motive was compassion for their weakness and their sorrows. And if ignorance of everything which it is needful a ruler should know is likely to do so much harm in the governing classes of the future, why is it, they ask reasonably enough, that such ignorance in the governing classes of the past had not been viewed with equal horror? . . .

Again, *this sceptical minority asks* the clergy to think whether it is really want of education which keeps the masses away from their min-istrations—whether the most completely educated men are not as open to reproach on this score as the workmen; and whether, perchance, this may not indicate that it is not education which lies at the bottom of this matter?

Once more, *those people,* whom there is no pleasing, *venture to doubt* whether the glory, which rests upon being able to undersell all the rest of the world, is a very safe kind of glory—whether we may not purchase it too dear; especially if we allow education, which ought to be directed to the making of men, to be diverted into a process of manufacturing hu-man tools, wonderfully adroit in the exercise of some technical industry, but good for nothing else.

And finally, *these people inquire* whether it is the masses alone who need a reformed and improved education. . . . They seem to think that the noble foundations of our old universities are hardly fulfilling their functions. . . . And while as zealous for education as the rest, they affirm that if the education of the richer classes were such as to fit them to be the leaders and governors of the poorer; and if the education of the poorer classes were such as to enable them to appreciate really wise guidance and good governance, the *politicians* need not *fear* mob-law, nor the *clergy lament* their want of flocks, nor the *capitalists prognosticate* the annihilation of the prosperity of the country.

Thomas H. Huxley, *Collected Essays*

We have now discussed four tools of style: transitional devices, key terms, hook-and-eye links, and parallel repeats. If you learn to employ these skillfully, you will be able to avoid the rough, jouncing style common to beginning writers and to achieve a sentence flow that will make your writing easy to follow and understand.

OBSERVATION EXERCISE

The passages below are the work of seasoned writers. Study them carefully for sentence flow, underlining and identifying the instances you find of transitional devices, repetition of key terms, hook-and-eye links, and parallel repeats.

1. A speaker commands resources of expression far richer than those of a writer. He can reinforce particular points by giving special emphasis of voice and intonation to them; he can make use of facial gestures. He can play tricks with his hands and fingers, opening and shutting them, waving them up and down and sideways. If he is near enough to his victim, he can even nudge him to drive home a specially important sally, although modern ideas of good manners tend to look on this practice as low-bred.

Adapted from Hugh Sykes Davies, *Grammar Without Tears*

2. Fifty years ago people in this country believed that "love apples" (tomatoes) were poisonous, because everybody believed that love apples were poisonous. This superstition, like many others, died a natural death without causing any serious hardship. But when potatoes were first introduced in Russia, the peasants would not plant or eat them, because, they said, they were "devil's apples." The rulers realized that the potato could become an important factor in agricultural economy; so they tried to overcome the peasants' reluctance by *forcing* them to eat potatoes. The question how to verify the assertion "potatoes are devil's apples" never arose. The peasants said it was "true," and the officials said it was "false." This controversy caused a great deal of unhappiness.

Anatol Rapoport, *Science and the Goals of Man*

3. How does it happen that children in general learn their mother-tongue so well? That this is a problem becomes clear when we contrast a child's first acquisition of its mother-tongue with the later acquisition of any foreign tongue. The contrast is indeed striking and manifold: here we have a quite little child, without experience or prepossessions: there

a bigger child, or it may be a grown-up person with all sorts of knowledge and powers: here a haphazard method of procedure; there the
whole task laid out in a system . . . : here no professional teachers, but
chance parents, brothers and sisters, nursery-mates and playmates; there
teachers trained for many years specially to teach languages: here only
oral instruction; there not only that, but reading-books, dictionaries,
and other assistance. And yet this is the result: here complete and exact
command of the language as a native speaks it, however stupid the children; there, in most cases, even with people otherwise highly gifted, a
defective and inexact command of language. On what does this difference depend?

Otto Jespersen, *Language: Its Nature, Development and Origin*

4. Man is a rational animal—so at least I have been told. Throughout
a long life, I have looked diligently for evidence in favor of this statement, but so far I have not had the good fortune to come across it,
though I have searched in many countries spread over three continents.
On the contrary, I have seen the world plunging continually further
into madness. I have seen great nations, formerly leaders of civilization,
led astray by preachers of bombastic nonsense. I have seen cruelty, per-
secution, and superstition increasing by leaps and bounds, until we have
almost reached the point where praise of rationality is held to mark a
man as an old fogey regrettably surviving from a bygone age. All this is
depressing, but gloom is a useless emotion. In order to escape from it,
I have been driven to study the past with more attention than I had
formerly given to it, and have found, as Erasmus found, that folly is
perennial and yet the human race has survived. The follies of our times
are easier to bear when they are seen against a background of past
follies.

Bertrand Russell, "An Outline of Intellectual Rubbish," *Unpopular Essays*

5. Some forms of ineffective thinking are due to our not unnatural
desire to have confident beliefs about complicated matters with regard
to which we must take some action or other. We are sometimes too lazy,
usually too busy, and often too ignorant to think out what is involved
in the statements we so readily accept. Few true statements about a
complicated state of affairs can be expressed in a single sentence. Our
need to have definite beliefs to hold onto is great; the difficulty in mas-
tering the evidence upon which such beliefs ought to be based is burdensome; consequently, we easily fall into the habit of accepting
compressed statements which save us from the trouble of thinking. Thus
arises what I shall call "Potted Thinking."

L. Susan Stebbing, *Thinking to Some Purpose*

6. Language is nothing but a set of human habits, the purpose of
which is to give expression to thoughts and feelings, and especially to

impart them to others. As with other habits it is not to be expected that they should be perfectly consistent. No one can speak exactly the same as everybody else or speak exactly in the same way under all circumstances and at all moments, hence a good deal of vacillation here and there. The divergencies would certainly be greater if it were not for the fact that the chief purpose of language is to make oneself understood by other members of the same community; this presupposes and brings about a more or less complete agreement on all essential points. The closer and more intimate the social life of a community is, the greater will be the concordance in speech between its members. In old times, when communication between various parts of the country was not easy and when the population was, on the whole, very stationary, a great many local dialects arose which differed very considerably from one another. . . . In recent times the enormously increased facilities of communication have to a great extent counteracted the tendency towards the splitting up of the language into dialects. . . .

Otto Jespersen, *Essentials of English Grammar*

7. Darwin's hypothesis as contained in his *Origin of Species* (1859) is known as the hypothesis of natural selection. This involves the idea that it is nature, or the environment, which selects those variants among the offspring that are to survive and reproduce. Darwin pointed out, first of all, that the parents of every species beget more offspring than can possibly survive. He maintained that, consequently, a struggle takes place among these offspring for food, shelter, warmth, and other conditions necessary for life. In this struggle certain individuals have the advantage because of the factor of *variation,* which means that no two of the offspring are exactly alike. Some are born strong, others weak; some have longer horns or sharper claws than their brothers and sisters or perhaps a coloration of body which enables them better to blend with their surroundings and thus to elude their enemies. It is these favored members of the species that win out in the struggle for existence; the others are eliminated generally before they have lived long enough to reproduce.

Edward M. Burns, *Western Civilizations,* 3rd ed.

REVISION PRACTICE

Rewrite the following sentences to achieve a smoother flow of thought. Use the devices suggested in parentheses.

1. In ancient Babylon much business was carried on near the gate of the city. A crowd of people chatting together and waiting for news from travelers could always be found there. (Hook-and-eye link)

2. Variety of pitch is another voice quality that is lacking in my speech delivery. The absence of this factor tends to make my speeches monotonous. (Key term)

3. In the course of college life one is constantly making new friends. One can hear of a rich variety of experiences from these new acquaintances during dormitory talk fests. (Key term and Hook-and-eye link)

4. The courses in the General Education program give students a broad and systematic basic knowledge. For example, in biological science they learn of life processes from the lowest forms up to man. They become acquainted with the music of the great composers of our Western tradition in the course called Exploring Music. The two courses in humanities teach them the history of Western Europe and acquaint them with important social and literary documents. (Parallel repeats)

5. An excellent way to learn to understand French is to listen to it in the language laboratory. You hear the language spoken easily and naturally by a native by means of the tapes there. You can listen by yourself and take all the time you want to master the lesson. (Hook-and-eye link and Transitional device)

6. One of the earlier Italian masters of painting and sculpture was Andrea Verrocchio. Leonardo da Vinci first learned the craft of painting from him. (Hook-and-eye link)

7. In the North of England travelers pass through the wild green mountains of Wordsworth's Lake District and up to the lowlands of Burns. They see the "checkered counties" of Housman in the West. The South reveals to them the heaths and moors made famous by Hardy. (Parallel repeats)

8. There are three things you should do in the introduction of your speech. You should capture the attention of your audience. This can be done in various ways, such as making a startling statement or telling a personal story or asking the audience a question. You should create a favorable impression toward yourself. This you can do by being natural and dignified and by treating your listeners with respect. You should lead into the body of your speech. A simple way to do this is to state your purpose. (Transitional devices)

9. This paper is divided into two sections for two reasons. First, it gives the reader some facts and figures on the advancements made in the field of jet aviation. Second, the last section of the paper was written for the purpose of informing the reader

when and where the first jet aircraft was invented. (Parallel repeats)

10. I had put off writing my term paper until the day before it was due. I had to sit up nearly all night to get it written in time for my eight o'clock class. (Transitional device)

ADDITIONAL REVISION PRACTICE

Rewrite the following sentences to achieve a smoother flow of thought. Use the devices suggested in parentheses.

1. The by-products of mankind's attempt to master science have been numerous. Our society has leisure time and industrial development never before experienced. (Repeat Key term "One by-product. . . .")

2. A good lecturer can hold the attention of the students. It is necessary to give vocal emphasis to important statements. Humor helps to break up the monotony of a class lecture. (Try two ways here: (1) Make passage into one sentence, using Parallel repeats in -ing. (2) Use Hook-and-eye at beginning of the second sentence—"To do"—and put the second and third sentences into one, using parallel repeats.)

3. The worst part about writing an in-class theme is getting organized. Some people get poor grades because they cannot organize their ideas. Students often give up in despair. (Use Hook-and-eye at the beginning of the second sentence and combine the last two into one. Avoid shift from "people" to "students.")

4. Survival is not merely a matter of keeping body and soul together, as it was in the jungle. You must keep within the good graces of your superiors. You must behave properly, which means putting up a courteous and hospitable front at all times. (Use Parallel repeat "It is a matter . . .")

5. Lincoln Highway is a road that runs east and west along the edge of the campus. North of Lincoln Highway, where it meets Castle Drive, are the Montgomery Arboretum and the Lagoon. There are houses on the south side. (Make change only in the third sentence.)

6. Lincoln Highway is like a broad river running along the campus and through the town. The banks of the river change color in the fall. The arboretum changes to yellow and orange as the frost kills the leaves. The leaves fall from the trees and

dye the road a dirty yellow. (Use Hook-and-eye at the beginning of the third sentence and combine last two sentences into one.)

2
DEVELOPING THOUGHT IN PARAGRAPHS

A paragraph is a block of print or writing that usually begins with an indentation and is built around a single topic or a single aspect of a topic. Thus each paragraph indentation will tell your readers that they have come to another topic, another aspect of the topic, or another division in thought.

Paragraphs vary in length from one word or phrase to hundreds of lines, and you may well wonder, "How long should I make my paragraphs?" A good answer lies at hand in your college textbooks of history, science, humanities, and the like. Open a few of them and see for yourself how long the paragraphs are. In normal expository prose you will probably find from one to three paragraph indentations on each printed page. Then a little word-counting and averaging will give you a rough clue to normal paragraph length.

But your main guide is the topic. A rather short topic might be dealt with in a single longish paragraph, whereas a longer topic may naturally break into several divisions, each deserving a paragraph by itself. Many students, beginning their composition course, fall into the error of using too many paragraphs. If you look at your theme and see a paragraph indentation every two or three lines, something is probably wrong. Either these paragraphs are not fully developed, or they should be regrouped into longer paragraphs.

A fully developed paragraph must say enough to clarify or explain its topic for your reader. The undeveloped paragraph leaves its generalization unsupported, unexplained. Here is an example of an undeveloped paragraph:

> One might ask *why I did not go to college in my hometown.* To answer this question is somewhat difficult, although I feel my reason is substantial. I know several graduates of City College, and few of them seem to have gotten anything out of their education.

This paragraph raises a question and leaves it in the air. The second sentence is a vague generalization, and the last sentence fails to give the "substantial reason" that the writer has promised.

Filling out paragraphs requires a good deal of practice in thought development. A helpful preliminary to this practice is reading some well-written paragraphs and tracing their patterns of thought development. In the following pages you will be given examples of some of the more useful patterns, which you may find profitable to imitate as you develop the various topics that confront you in your writing. The patterns are often given these names:

1. Example
2. Time arrangement
3. Space arrangement
4. General-and-specific
5. Statistics
6. Comparison-contrast
7. Division or classification
8. Cause-and-effect
9. Analogy

To this list we must add three qualifications. (1) There are more patterns than those listed. (2) The categories overlap. That is to say, you will meet with passages that may be classified according to two or more of the labels on the list. (3) You will come across sound and logical writing that does not seem to follow any identifiable pattern of development and yet is clear and cogent. Nevertheless, an acquaintance with these patterns will be valuable to you as you set about learning to write clear and simple prose.

Samples of Thought Development

1. DEVELOPMENT BY EXAMPLE

This is a very common and useful method of thought development. It is quite simple. The writer makes a statement and then uses one or more examples to illustrate, support, and make clear the statement. The order is sometimes reversed, proceeding from the examples to the statement they illustrate.

> *Topic 1* Compound superlatives in the language of the Ozarks.
> *Development* Numerous examples.

There are many compound superlatives in the language of the Ozarks, such as *loud-cussin'est, hell-raisin'est, fish-ketchin'est, vote-gettin'est,* and *rabbit-killin'est.* A man once told me, "Katy is the most *out-doin'est* woman that ever lived," and I think he meant that she was surprisingly vigorous and energetic. One of my friends was badly cut in a knife fight and required many stitches to repair his injuries; of the physician who did the work he remarked, "Doc Holton is the *stitch-takin'est* feller I ever met up with." A boatman who prepared meals for tourists on a float-trip was described as "the *pancake-cookin'est* feller on the creek." A man who sold out several times and moved to Oklahoma, invariably returning a few months later, was referred to as "the *back-comin'est* feller in this country." An editorial in a Little Rock newspaper points out that the United States is "the *statistics-keepingest* nation on the face of the earth." A certain senator in southwest Missouri was described as "the *potguttedest* candidate that ever crawled up on a stump." A mountain man remarked to me that his children were maturing very rapidly, adding, "I believe Lolly is the *growed-uppest* one of the lot." Such superlatives as *sleepy-headedest* and *high-poweredest* are familiar to everybody in the back hills.

Vance Randolph and George P. Wilson, *Down in the Holler*

Topic 2 Scientific generalizations are subject to change.
Development Use of a single hypothetical example.

A scientific generalization is always subject to change in the light of further evidence. As an example, let us see what could happen to Cuvier's famous generalization that all animals with both horns and hoofs eat grasses and grains, not flesh. Suppose that a scientist in South America has discovered a large plateau high among the mountains of the Andes. As he and his party begin to cross this plateau, they notice in the distance a herd of strange animals that seem to be grazing. Approaching more closely, they take out their binoculars and inspect the herd carefully. They note that these animals all have horns and hoofs. But they also discover, to their amazement, that instead of grazing, some of the animals are eating rabbits, which they have apparently killed. This evidence makes it necessary to change the generalization they had held—that *all* animals with horns and hoofs are granivorous, not carnivorous.

PRACTICE TOPICS FOR DEVELOPMENT BY EXAMPLES

1. I have learned a lot about study methods in the last month.
2. Haste makes waste.
3. Sports in high school are good for a student.
4. My hometown has much to be proud of.
5. Debating can be a valuable addition to a student's education.
6. Blind dating is hazardous.

7. Snowmobiles are useful but dangerous.
8. I have been surprised to see how, as I grow older, my father seems to get smarter.

2. DEVELOPMENT BY TIME ARRANGEMENT

When we tell a sequence of events in the order of their occurrence, we are using development by time. We frequently use this method in relating experiences and spinning yarns. Time order can be juggled around. For instance, you can begin with an exciting moment and then go back and show what led up to this moment.

Topic   History of the word *nice*.
Development   Changes in the meaning of *nice* during the passage of centuries.

The word *nice,* which today is a verbal factotum to indicate approval, has had a long and interesting history. We first meet it in Roman times as the Latin adjective *nescius,* which meant "not knowing" or igno- rant." Then, when the Roman armies invaded what is now France and when the Roman traders and settlers followed them, they naturally brought with them their native Latin tongue, including the word *nescius.* The speech of Rome became the speech of Gaul (France). In the course of centuries *nescius* changed in form and sound, and when we next meet it—in the twelfth century in the work of Chrétien de Troyes —it had become *nice,* pronounced like "niece." It had also taken on another meaning, that of "foolish." Next, the word *nice* entered England. We all remember the Norman Conquest of 1066, when the Norman French conquered England, and the period of French domina- tion that followed. During these centuries the French and English lan- guages existed side by side, and it was inevitable that many French words should become naturalized in English. One of these was *nice,* and it first appears in written records as an English word in the fourteenth century. Its meaning was "foolish," and it was regularly used in this sense by Chaucer, the great fourteenth-century poet. As time went on, its meaning narrowed to "foolishly particular about small things." From this meaning it was an easy step to the next one, "particular about small things," and hence "discriminating," "accurate." Thus one could speak of a "nice observer of human foibles" or a "nice taste in wine" or a "nice distinction." The final change in meaning was from "dis- criminating" to "agreeable" or "excellent." What a nice (discriminating) person with a nice (accurate) taste would choose would be a nice (ex- cellent) thing. This change appeared in the eighteenth century. The last two meanings of *nice* are in use today. Careful writers and speakers often use it to mean "discriminating," and everyone uses it in ordinary speech in the general sense of "agreeable" and "pleasant."

PRACTICE TOPICS FOR DEVELOPMENT BASED ON TIME SEQUENCE

1. The last days before graduation stand out clearly in my memory.
2. We took an unusual trip last summer.
3. Recently we had to pack up and move into a new house, all in one week.
4. A basketball player must keep to a strict schedule when preparing for the season.
5. You cannot imagine the trouble I had getting a book out of the library.
6. It took three weeks to plan our vacation trip.
7. You must begin preparing for a party several days in advance.

3. DEVELOPMENT BY SPACE ARRANGEMENT

Here you take your reader from one place or position to another in an orderly fashion. You would use this method if you were to describe such things as a college campus or your room or a pencil or a dime.

Topic English words have different meanings in different parts of the world.

Development Details are arranged in the spatial order of England, Australia, South Africa, and the United States.

The words and expressions that constitute the word stock of the English language differ considerably in different parts of the English-speaking world. In England, for example, the motor of a car is under a *bonnet,* not a *hood,* and the riders in the front seat are protected from the wind by a *windscreen.* An Englishman will do *straightaway* what an American will do *right away.* One rides the *Underground* in London, not the *subway.* A well-dressed man may be wearing a *bowler* (derby), and he holds up his socks not his trousers with his *suspenders.* In Australia one hears the term *dinky-di* in place of our OK. What is a *ranch* to us is a *station* to an Australian. The character that we know as a *hobo* or *tramp* is known in the continent down under as a *swagman* or *swaggie.* He travels through the *outback* or *bush* (back country) and carries his *swag* (bundle). In South Africa, English has acquired many new words, especially from the local variety of Dutch called Afrikaans. A village is known as a *dorp.* An overseer or foreman is a *bass,* a Dutch word that was independently adopted into American English in the form of *boss.* A hill is a *kopje,* a word that we meet in John Masefield's famous poem, "A Consecration," in the form of *koppie.* A movie is a *bioscope,* a wagon trip is a *trek,* and a porch is a *stoep,* which also appears in the United States as *stoop.* In the United States we find local differences in the word stock. In Boston, for instance, one drinks *tonic,* whereas in Chicago the same beverage is *pop*. When a woman takes her husband to work in the family car, she *carries* him to work in Texas and *drives* him to work in Iowa. A *fried cake* in upper New York state is a *cruller* in New Jersey and a *doughnut* in Minneapolis. The plural of *you* is *you-all* throughout the South, but in western Pennsylvania it becomes *you'ns*. We see, then, that the vocabulary of the English language is not uniform, but is different wherever we go.

PRACTICE TOPICS FOR DEVELOPMENT BY SPATIAL ARRANGEMENT

1. The Mustang has an unusual instrument panel.
2. My father's workshop shows how meticulous he is.
3. My room is arranged to suit my special needs.
4. When I can afford it, I'm going to have a perfect stereo system.
5. Our campus is easy to get around once you understand its layout.
6. Our college library is well-planned for browsing.
7. My state has a wide variety of scenic interests.
8. New York is easy to get around in.

4. DEVELOPMENT BY GENERAL-AND-SPECIFIC

Here you have a choice of two procedures. (1) You may begin with a general statement and continue by presenting specific details that bear out, expand, and support the general statement. This order is illustrated in the first example below. (2) You may reverse this order, mentioning the specifics first and then tying them together with the generalization at the end. This reversed order is shown in the second example.

Topic 1 The American office as a temple of status.
Development Listing of specific details.

The American office is a veritable temple of status. Though they may seem almost imperceptible, the symbols are manifested everywhere. Some have a useful purpose—the memo pad "From the desk of . . ."; the routing slip (Should the names on the memorandum be listed by seniority or alphabetically?); who sits with whom in the company dining room. Others are rooted in propriety; who can call whom by nickname, at what level may people smoke? To what grade of washroom is one entitled? Is the office carpeted or does he rate only linoleum? Some are rooted in functions only marginal: the facsimile signature stamp, for example—evidence that a man's importance is such that he must write to a great number of people, even if he doesn't use the facsimile signature in doing it. All these are favorite topics of office humor, of course, but as the fact itself is witness, the symbols communicate.

Adapted from William H. Whyte, Jr., *Is Anybody Listening?*

Topic 2 The effectiveness of written style as compared with colloquial style.

Development Description of an experiment—its method, conditions, subjects—and a resultant generalization.

A British professor recently conducted a revealing experiment in language. He constructed a short message and arranged the words in two different ways. One was an arrangement characteristic of written style; it went like this:

He's doing research on the procedures for assessing, the methods of surveying, and the techniques for exploiting the mineral resources of various parts of the Commonwealth.

The second arrangement was a colloquial one, that is, characteristic of spoken style. It contained the same information and the same words:

He's doing research on the mineral resources of the various parts of the Commonwealth—the procedures for assessing, the methods of surveying, and the techniques for exploiting them.

These two arrangements were tested out on two groups of undergraduates, who had no idea of what was involved. Each group consisted of about thirty-five first-and-second-year students, in roughly equal proportions. The two forms of the test piece occupied the same reading time, and the reading rate was very fast, as a final check against one hundred percent perception and recall that would, of course, give data not susceptible of comparison. The group that received the written style absorbed on average *forty-five* percent of the information. But the group that received the colloquial style absorbed on average *sixty* percent of the information. It might seem, then, if we can generalize from so simple a case and from so few numbers, that the arrangement of words which a speaker uses can influence the retention of what he says.

Adapted from Randolph Quirk,
"Colloquial English and Communication," in *Studies in Communication*

PRACTICE TOPICS FOR DEVELOPMENT BY PROCEEDING
FROM GENERAL TO SPECIFIC OR SPECIFIC TO GENERAL

1. You can recognize a New Yorker anywhere.
2. A used car is expensive for a student.
3. The assignments in this course could be improved.
4. Love conquers all.
5. A college student has a busy life.
6. Being in college brings new responsibilities.

5. DEVELOPMENT BY STATISTICS

In this method a conclusion is supported by figures and statistics. This method can also bear other labels, such as development from general to specific or from specific to general, depending on the position of the conclusion.

Topic English is an important language.
Development Statistics on the number of speakers of English 400 years ago and in our time.

English is an important language. Only 400 years ago it was spoken by fewer than 5 million persons living on a small island off the coast of Europe. Today it spans the globe. On the original island it is now the tongue of some 50 million people. In Canada it is spoken by 17 million. In the United States an estimated 210 million use English as their daily language. Away down under in Australia, over 14 million persons have their cockney brand of English. To these figures we must add the Englishmen scattered over the earth, the Irish, and the many Europeans to whom English is a second tongue. Thus we see that there are probably over 400 million speakers of English. And when we add to this the fact that it is the language of the most powerful and technologically advanced country in the world, we can harbor no doubt that English is an important language.

PRACTICE TOPICS FOR DEVELOPMENT BY USE OF STATISTICS

1. Federal aid to education is decreasing.
2. Lower speed limits have reduced highway deaths.
3. The average age at which couples marry is changing.
4. The Women's Liberation Movement has improved the status of women.
5. Inflation is imperiling the existence of small colleges.
6. Divorces are on the increase in our country.
7. Major crimes are a growing threat to our citizens.
8. The United States is improving in its ability to be the bread basket of the world.
9. In many sports in our country, blacks excel over whites.

(Note: Almanacs are an excellent source of statistics.)

6. DEVELOPMENT BY COMPARISON-CONTRAST

You can develop a comparison by pointing out similar features. You could compare the United States and Russia in terms of size, climate, political influence, economic power. You can develop a contrast by pointing out differences between things somewhat similar. You would contrast the United States and Russia, or California and Rhode Island, but certainly not a goldfish and a flower pot. Both comparison and contrast might be used in the same theme.

In general, there are two methods of developing a comparison. (1) Describe one side of the comparison as fully as you intend and then deal entirely with the other side. When you practice this method, be sure to follow the same order of points of comparison for each side. The first example that follows shows this method. When you use the first method, be sure your transitions are clear. (2) Compare the two activities point by point, as shown in the second example that follows.

Topic 1 Differences between high school and college life.
Development The details of high school life are all given first; then a description of college life is presented.

High school life and college life have startling differences. In high school my teachers were always harassing me about the quality of my work and about late or unfinished papers. I seemed to have all the time I needed for extracurricular activities. My mother's good meals, my own quiet room, and all my pals at East High I took for granted. In college, my life suddenly became different. The responsibility for quality work and for promptness in handing in my papers was left strictly up to me. The first college year has left me little time for outside activities, and I have had to budget my time carefully. The cafeteria meals, my noisy room, and my new friends are all a contrast to my previous life. Thoughts of home life sometimes keep me awake at night after the clamor of the dormitory has subsided. However, each new day with its challenges, excitement, and independence brings stimulation that makes memories of high school life seem dull indeed.

Topic 2 Reading and listening as means of learning.
Development Point-by-point comparison.

The two communicative skills of reading and listening, research tells us, are about equally effective as means of learning. But from the point of view of the receptor, reading is sometimes better. *Reading* has the advantage of being much *faster* than listening. An average normal rate for an adult reader is perhaps 300 words a minute, although many can exceed this by a good deal. In listening, however, one's rate is held down to that of the speaker, from about 125 or 175 words a minute. In *reading* we can *set our own pace,* taking it fast or slowly as we wish; and when we're tired, we can take a break. But in listening we must take the pace set for us by the speaker. If it is too slow for our condition of alertness, we may tend to daydream; and if it is too fast for the difficulty of the material, we may become fatigued and lose the thread of thought. When we are *reading, we can* always *stop* to reread a difficult passage, and we have all the time we want to look up things that will help us understand what we are reading. Listening, however, is another story.

We must catch everything on the fly or else it is lost. If our attention wanders even for a few seconds, we may miss an important sentence that is a key to what follows.

PRACTICE TOPICS FOR DEVELOPMENT BY COMPARISON-CONTRAST

1. A doctor is more valuable to the community than a lawyer.
2. A typewriter is more useful than a tape recorder.
3. Traveling by train is more fun than flying.
4. Regular study brings better results than periodic cramming.
5. Basketball is a more demanding game than tennis.
6. Our popular music is in some ways like the music of the Roaring Twenties.
7. My math course makes different demands on me than does my English course.
8. The ability to speak persuasively is worth more than the ability to reason.
9. The library is a better place to study than the dorm.
10. The Midwest is more friendly than the East.

7. DEVELOPMENT BY DIVISION OR CLASSIFICATION

In using this method, you first divide the topic or main point into several parts. Then you develop each part in turn, using any of the methods we are dealing with here. In the selection that follows, notice that the topic is divided into four parts, each of which is developed by examples.

> *Topic* Making new words.
> *Development* Dividing the material into four groups. (In a long paragraph like the following, it is sometimes helpful to number the divisions of the topic.)

In English there are four ways in which new words can be made: by composition, by derivation, by sound-symbolism, and by root-juncture. The first one, composition, means the joining together of two existing words to form a compound word. From this process we have got thousands of compound words, such as *cherry tree, blackbird, dark red, breakfast, overcome.* In the most frequent kind of compound word, the last part of the word has a general meaning that is made more specific by the first part, as in *racehorse, horse race, doghouse,* and *house dog.* Other kinds of compound words are so many and the relationships between their parts so complex that it would not be profitable to explore the subject in our limited space. Derivation means making a new word by adding a meaningful prefix or suffix to an already existing word. As examples of words made by the addition of a prefix, we may cite *intramural, counteract, impossible, coexist, intercollegiate.* Words that have

been made by the addition of a suffix may be exemplified by *hoggish,
goodness, draftee, waiter, waitress, cigarette, lemonade, noisy,* and
sweetly. The number of meaningful suffixes available in English for
derivation greatly exceeds the number of prefixes. Sound-symbolism
means the inventing of a new word in which the sounds in it resemble
its meaning. Words like *sizzle, Ping-Pong, bang, roar, thump, seesaw,
bobwhite, slurp* are common examples of sound symbolism. The process
is an active one, as are the two mentioned above, and observant students
will find many instances if they listen carefully to the language around
them, especially slang. Root-juncture means the formation of a new
word by joining together two roots, usually from the Latin or Greek.
Biology, for example, is formed from two Greek-derived roots—*bio,*
meaning life, and *-ology,* meaning a theory or a science or a doctrine.
Thus biology is the science of life. Other examples of root-junctures are
*audiophile, telephone, anthropology, phonograph, gramophone, circum-
spect, introvert.* Today this method of forming new words is used largely
in science.

PRACTICE TOPICS FOR DEVELOPMENT BY DIVISION OR CLASSIFICATION

1. The animals that make the best pets for children are dogs, rabbits,
   and squirrels.
2. After attending classes at college for several weeks, I have discovered
   four sure ways of identifying a dull teacher.
3. While working in a library, I learned that there are four classes of
   library visitors: those who come to look for a date, those who come
   to read the magazines, those who rush in to cram for an hour at the
   reserve shelf before a quiz, and those who are interested only in taking out books.
4. A visitor to my hometown will find at least three kinds of entertainment.
5. In my dormitory there are three kinds of students who, I believe, are
   getting the most out of college: These are the Bookworm, the Social
   Butterfly, and the Activities Chaser.

8. DEVELOPMENT BY CAUSE-AND-EFFECT

Here you have a choice of two procedures: (1) Describe a situation
and then show what has caused it. This is done in the first illustrative paragraph. (2) Deal with the causes first and then present the
effects or results stemming from these causes. The second example
shows this procedure.

> *Topic 1* The problems the college freshman faces in learn-
> ing to speak before a group.

Development The problems of the freshman speaker are listed and the causes are described.

The college freshman who is learning to speak before a group is sometimes ineffective at first and is unable to convey to the group exactly the message or point that he is trying to make. And he is frequently surprised to find out that his listeners did not grasp the point, for it seemed perfectly clear to him. This ineffectiveness is usually caused by three difficulties, each of which can be overcome with practice and care. The first is that the speaker does not give extra emphasis to the important parts of his talk. Instead, everything that he is putting forth rolls along flatly and without variation; there are no hills and plains. The consequence of this unrelieved sameness is that listeners have trouble in separating the important from the unimportant, the significant from the trivial; and at the end they are unsure of the point. The second difficulty is that the speaker does not set up signposts along the way. He forgets, for instance, to number his points. He forgets to pause between points. He forgets to use relational expressions to show thought relationships—such expressions as *in the first place, as a beginning; on the other hand, on the contrary, nevertheless; in addition, to continue, next; hence, thus, consequently; for example, for instance, to illustrate; to conclude, in conclusion, in short, finally, to summarize, then.* Without such signposts, listeners sometimes get lost, and then they lose interest and begin to think about other things. The final difficulty is that the beginner's rate of speed is far too rapid. In his nervousness and in his desire to get along with his subject, he speeds ahead at a pace that makes listening difficult. And when listening becomes difficult, listeners tend to give up. These three difficulties are the cause of much of the ineffectiveness of talks given by beginning speakers before college groups.

Topic 2 Dangers freshman students face in beginning college work.
Development Some of the causes of freshman difficulties are discussed, leading to an obvious result.

The dangers faced by freshman students as they begin their college work can have disastrous results. If they have not learned to study effectively, they may spend hours on what should be a reasonably short reading assignment. They may fail to budget their time and discover that the day is too short for all they must cram into it. They may let themselves be enticed into social programs and college activities to the extent that there is insufficient time left for the demanding work of the classroom and laboratory. The result is that, at the end of the semester, they receive a "Dear John" letter from the dean indicating that they must leave college to make room for more promising students.

PRACTICE TOPICS FOR DEVELOPMENT BY CAUSE-TO-EFFECT OR EFFECT-TO-CAUSE

1. The increasing use of bicycles is beneficial to society.
2. There is a great need for more public, noncommercial television.
3. Rock bands (or beards, or indelicate language) are popular among the young.
4. What are the common causes of academic failure among college freshmen?
5. A poor examination grade may be explained in several ways.
6. Failure to obey traffic laws can be dangerous.
7. A college student should learn to type.
8. Many people have given up smoking today.

9. DEVELOPMENT BY ANALOGY

An analogy is a special kind of comparison. The items compared are usually things that one considers quite unlike in most respects, such as an automobile engine and the human body, a garden and a college, a house and a book. An analogy often proceeds, point by point, for considerable length.

Topic The structure of a book.
Development Similarities between the architecture of a house and the structure of a book are discussed.

A book is like a single house. It is a mansion of many rooms—rooms on different levels, of different sizes and shapes, with different outlooks, rooms with different functions to perform. These rooms are independent, in part. Each has its own structure and interior decoration. But they are not absolutely independent and separate. They are connected by doors and arches, by corridors and stairways. Because they are connected, the partial function which each performs contributes its share to the usefulness of the whole house. Otherwise the house would not be genuinely livable.

The architectural analogy is almost perfect. A good book, like a good house, is an orderly arrangement of parts. Each major part has a certain amount of independence. As we shall see, it may have an interior structure of its own. But it must also be connected with the other parts—that is, related to them functionally—for otherwise it could not contribute its share to the intelligibility of the whole.

As houses are more or less livable, so books are more or less readable. The most readable book is an architectural achievement on the part of the author. The best books are those that have the most intelligible structure and, I might add, the most apparent.

Mortimer Adler, *How to Read a Book*

PRACTICE TOPICS FOR DEVELOPMENT BY ANALOGY
1. The human life cycle is like the four seasons.
2. The human heart is like a fuel pump.
3. A college is like a supermarket (or an automobile-production plant).
4. College life is like a window-shopping tour (a trackmeet, a bridge, a lottery, a game of cards, a river).
5. A college freshman is like a rat in a maze.
6. Learning a foreign language is like learning to play golf.
7. Saturday night in the dorm is like winter on the prairie.
8. Starting college is like learning to swim.

PRACTICE IN THOUGHT DEVELOPMENT

An entire theme can be developed by using only one of the methods of thought development as well as by using several. Write a short theme on one of the titles below or on one of your choice. Label in the margin the method or methods of thought development that you are using. You may discover other ways of developing thought, for example, by reasons or by definition. If so, feel free to use them, but give each a label.

1. Desirable Methods of Protest
2. On Working Your Way Through College
3. On Learning to Study Efficiently
4. On Becoming a Skilful Hang-Glider
5. Fact and Fiction About Black Students
6. Achieving Maturity
7. My Need for a Larger Budget
8. Finding a Place to Live
9. Getting Married While in College
10. Finding Time for All I Want to Do
11. A Chicano's Chance in Life

3
ORGANIZING BY OUTLINE

The scratch outline described in the beginning of this book is usually all you need in preparing to write a short informal theme. But as your theme assignments grow longer and more complex, you may find it handy to learn how to make a more careful and detailed outline. Though at first this may seem merely an added chore, it will really save you time and should result in better themes and grades.

An outline is the ground plan for a piece of writing. It consists of a series of sentences or topics in an orderly sequence and grouping. Practice in outlining is useful to a writer because it increases skill in organizing ideas.

Your outline helps you to arrange your main points in order, to group supporting material under the proper main points, and to place the parts you wish to emphasize in the most strategic positions.

Your outlines for papers will often be short and simple. If, for example, you prepare an outline of a short theme, it may be a simple one like this:

CENTRAL IDEA: *Underlining is a valuable study aid to a college student.*

1. *Underlining forces you to think.*
   a. It helps you find main points.
   b. It shows the thought structure of the assigned reading.
   c. It helps you to associate examples and supporting material with the right points.
2. *Underlining enables you to review quickly before an examination.*
   a. You can quickly locate the most important general statements and ideas.
   b. You can see at once what supporting material you need to restudy.

This outline contains your two main points supporting the central idea and the supporting subpoints under each main point—all in the order in which you intend to present them. Notice that each item is a full sentence. Using full sentences in an outline helps you in one important respect: it shows you that you have definite *points* to discuss, not just vague topics. But, if you choose, you may use topics instead of sentences. Here is a topic outline that you might use for a short paper:

CENTRAL IDEA: *Knowing how to review will give you better examination grades.*

1. *How to review alone*
   a. Finding the organization of each block of reading
   b. Finding the major points (ideas or general statements)
   c. Filling in with supporting points or details
   d. Correlating class notes with reading

2. *How to review with a classmate*
   a. Deciding what is most important
   b. Finding relationship of most important points
   c. Questioning each other and verifying answers
   d. Comparing class notes

An outline is a private affair. No one sees it but the writer because it is just a means to an end, the end of whipping your material into a logical and effective shape. Therefore, you do not have to be fussy about most matters of form—punctuation, capital letters, the system of numbering and lettering, and so on. One matter of form, however, does require careful attention: all items in the same sequence of numbers or letters should be in parallel form; that is, they should have the same grammatical structure. Parallel form guards your organization. It helps you to make sure that the ideas you have grouped together really belong together, and it keeps you from straying off on an irrelevant point. As an example, let us look again at point 2 of the outline above, with one item thrown out of parallel form:

2. *How to review with a classmate*
   a. Deciding what is most important
   b. Finding relationship of most important points
   c. Questioning each other and verifying answers
   d. Class notes

In this numbered sequence, *class notes* is not parallel; it is a noun, and the three other items begin with verbals indicating an action. Now, with the term *class notes* in your outline, the question for you as a writer is, "What about class notes?" What are you going to say about them? Will you tell how illegible they are? Will you describe the evident omissions? Will you advise your readers to query the lecturer about doubtful points? If you do any of these things, you will be straying off into an irrelevancy, and your readers will notice this at once. But if your outline form is parallel—*d. Comparing class notes*—you will know that you are to write about an action that you and your classmate will engage in, an action that is in line with the three previous actions—*deciding, finding,* and *questioning.* Moreover, your readers will perceive that you are adding a fourth point that is parallel in idea with the preceding three.

If your outline is really going to assist you in planning a paper, it must be specific, informative, and full. Such an outline will channel your thoughts smoothly from beginning to end, and you can then concentrate on filling in details and making effective transitions. The usefulness of an outline that is specific, informative, and full can easily be demonstrated. Below, you will find two outlines for a paper on this central idea: "I plan to be a primary teacher." The first one, you will see, is vague and barren, and would be of little assistance to you in preparing your paper. When you read the second one, compare it point by point with the first.

FIRST OUTLINE

1. *Introduction*
   a. What my friends say
   b. How I react toward children
2. *Why go into teaching?*
   a. Service to community
   b. Work
   c. World
   d. Vacations
3. *Why avoid teaching?*
   a. Work
   b. Money
4. *Conclusion*

SECOND OUTLINE

  I. *My interest in teaching*
   A. My friends say it is personally satisfying
   B. I like children
 II. *Rewards of teaching*
   A. Opportunity for useful service
      1. Character is formed in early grades
      2. Habits leading to later success are acquired in first two grades
   B. Regular employment
   C. Chance to see world
      1. Primary schools exist in all the civilized world
      2. Government opportunities to teach abroad
         a. In military services
         b. On exchange program
         c. In noncontinental U.S.
      3. Chance to meet people
         a. Will meet many people while traveling
   D. Long vacations
III. *Disadvantages of teaching*
   A. Tiring work and long hours

    B. Low pay and retirement benefits
    C. Primary jobs are scarce today
  IV. *Rewards exceed disadvantages*

The second outline is beginning to look usable; it is more specific, informative, and full. But before you begin to write from it, you had better look at it with a critical mind and ask a few key questions.

1. Do I have a reasonable and effective order to my points? As we look at the outline, we notice that the major point seems to be "Rewards of teaching" and that this is in the center, which is not a position of emphasis. Wouldn't it be better to follow the introductory first point with "Disadvantages of teaching"? You could lead into it with a transitional sentence like, "It is true, of course, that a teaching career does have some disadvantages." Then, after discussing these disadvantages, you could move to your major point as the culminating section, using a transitional sentence such as, "Though teaching has its disadvantages, it also offers rich rewards."

2. Do I have enough to say about each point? As we study the outline, two points seem rather thin: "Regular employment" and "Long vacations." Neither has any subpoints, and there really isn't much to say about either one. Perhaps they could be combined into one: "Regular employment with long vacations." Now the point is a little more substantial.

3. When I use subpoints, are there always at least two? The reason for the requirement of at least two subpoints is a logical one: you cannot divide anything into fewer than two parts. If, then, you have only one subpoint, it is probable that it should be subsumed under the point above. Looking at the outline, we find one point, "Chance to meet people," that has only one subpoint, "Will meet many people while traveling." So let us combine them in this way: "Chance to meet people while traveling."

This is how the outline will look:

CENTRAL IDEA: *I plan to be a primary-school teacher.*

  I. *My interest in teaching*
    A. My friends say it is personally satisfying
    B. I like children
  II. *Disadvantages of teaching*
    A. Tiring work and long hours
    B. Low pay and retirement benefits
    C. Primary jobs are scarce today

III. *Rewards of teaching*
    A. Opportunity for useful service
        1. Character is formed in early grades
        2. Habits leading to later success are acquired in early grades
    B. Regular employment with long vacations
    C. Chance to see world
        1. Primary schools exist in all the civilized world
        2. Government opportunities to teach abroad
            a. In military services
            b. On exchange program
            c. In noncontinental U.S.
        3. Chance to meet people while traveling
IV. *Rewards exceed disadvantages*

Here at last is a usable outline. However, it is still imperfect: it mixes topics with sentences; point IV is not in parallel form; and under point III, point C3 does not seem quite in line with points C1 and C2. Of these three imperfections, the third one may give you trouble, for it is a logical matter. The difficulty is that the *idea* here is not logically parallel with those of C1 and C2, which are both concerned with chances to get jobs; and in writing you might be hard put to make your social plan in C3 fit in with the two preceding points on getting a job. There are two solutions to your difficulty. One is to remove point C3, for you still have enough material for your paper. The other is to recast the whole of point C, which could go something like this:

    C. Chance to see the world
        1. Job opportunities
            a. Primary schools exist in all the civilized world
            b. Government opportunities to teach abroad
                (1) In military services
                (2) On exchange program
                (3) In noncontinental U.S.
        2. Cultural benefits
            a. Meet people through travel and see how they live
            b. See famous places

Now you have a logical structure, one in which you can easily make a transition from C1 to C2. You can safely ignore the other imperfections in the outline, which are merely formal, and go ahead with the writing. And with such an outline—logical, specific, informative, and full—the job of writing is already half-done.

Let us now start from the beginning and see how an outline is built, step by step. We shall assume that you, a college student, have received a letter from the English 12 class of your hometown high school. A number of the class are going to college next year, and they are getting worried about the hazards of college work. So they have asked you to write an article for the school paper on what they should do in English 12 to get ready for freshman English and for college classes in general. This is a golden opportunity for you. Now you must get to work laying your ground plan. And here are the four stages you will probably go through to prepare a usable outline for what you hope will be a dazzling article.

Stage 1. The first thing to do is to get your ideas down. Their form and order do not matter yet, for they are only your raw material. Just get them down as they come to your mind. After half an hour of scribbling, you have a list that will look something like this:

1. Better learn to *use* your language.
2. Using language is more important than knowing about literature.
3. College reading is stiff.
4. To read well, you should know how to underline and take notes.
5. You've got to remember what's in your reading assignments.
6. Writing standards are high.
7. Better know spelling and punctuation before coming to college.
8. Learn how to write exposition; it's the most important and the hardest.
9. Know good usage for writing.
10. Organizing your papers.
11. Practice with paragraphs.
12. Reading—ask yourself key questions and answer them, and tell someone exactly what you have read.
13. College writing should be accurate—say what you mean.
14. Speaking is learned through practice—get it now.
15. Colleges require public speaking.
16. College writing must be clear at first reading.
17. Must learn to listen to lectures.
18. Must learn to remember what you hear in lectures—important things, that is.
19. Must learn to take notes on lectures.
20. In speaking, organize your talk.
21. Self-confidence through speaking.
22. Learn to deliver a speech smoothly.

23. Speaking will help you to get into debate.
24. Writing will help you get on the college paper.
25. Recreational reading.
26. Much information gotten through college lectures.
27. Freshman composition is required everywhere, of all freshmen.
28. Practice reading hard stuff now.
29. Learn to outline what you read to get general organization.
30. Students fail on account of poor writing.
31. Much writing practice is needed in high school.
32. Learn to write connected sentences.

Stage 2.   Now you must find a central idea for your article and sort your raw material into groups. At the same time, you may want to tidy up the wording of some items, and you can add anything new that you think of. When you have completed this stage, your material will probably look like this:

CENTRAL IDEA: *Learn to use your language.*

READING

1. College reading is stiff.
2. To read well, you should know how to underline and take notes.
3. You must remember what's in your reading assignments.
4. Ask yourself key questions and answer them.
5. Tell someone exactly what you have read.
6. Recreational reading.
7. Practice reading solid stuff now.
8. Learn to outline for organization.

WRITING

1. Writing standards are high.
2. Better know spelling and punctuation before coming to college.
3. Learn to write exposition; very important and hard.
4. Know good usage.
5. Organize your papers.
6. Practice with paragraphs.
7. College writing must be accurate; you must be able to say what you mean.
8. College writing must be clear.
9. Writing will help you get on staff of college paper.
10. Freshman composition is required everywhere of freshmen.
11. Students fail because of poor writing.
12. Much writing practice needed in high school.
13. Learn to write connected sentences.

SPEAKING

1. Speaking is learned through practice; get it now.
2. Colleges require public speaking.
3. Organize your talk.
4. Develop self-confidence in speaking.
5. Deliver speech smoothly.
6. Speaking will help you get into debate.

LISTENING

1. You must learn to listen to lectures.
2. You must learn to remember what is important in lectures.
3. You must learn to take good lecture notes.
4. Much information is gained through classroom lectures.

EXTRAS

1. Using language is more important than knowing about literature.

Stage 3. Now comes the hard work. In each group you must find a reasonable order for your ideas. You must sift out your main points, get them in order, and list the subpoints under them, so far as you can do it at this stage. You can also continue to improve your wording and can add anything further that you happen to remember. When this stage is completed—and it's the hardest one—your article will be taking shape. Here is how it might look at stage three:

CENTRAL IDEA: *You should develop your language skills in high school.*

1. *Reading*
   a. College reading is difficult.
   b. You must remember what you have read.
   c. You should practice with solid reading now.
   d. Learn to underline and take notes.
   e. Learn to outline for organization.
   f. Learn to ask key questions and answer them.
   g. Retell to others what you read.
   h. Recreational reading???
2. *Writing*
   a. Freshman composition is required in many colleges.
   b. Writing standards in college are high.
      (1) You should know spelling, punctuation, and good usage before coming.
      (2) Many students fail because of poor writing.

(3) College writing must be accurate.

(4) College writing must be clear.

   c. You should get much writing practice in high school.

     (1) Exposition is most important.

     (2) Practice writing different kinds of paragraphs.

     (3) Organize each paragraph, with beginning, middle, and end.

     (4) Learn to connect your sentences with transitions.

   d. Writing will help you get on college paper.

3. *Speaking*

   a. Colleges often require public speaking of freshmen.

   b. Get speaking practice now.

     (1) Gives you self-confidence.

     (2) Gives you smooth delivery, free from common faults.

     (3) Gives you practice in organization.

     (4) May help you get on debate team???

4. *Listening*

   a. Much learning is gained from classroom lectures.

   b. You must and can learn to listen effectively to lectures.

   c. Learn to remember what is important—main points and their connections.

   d. Learn to take good lecture notes while listening.

Stage 4. Here you do the final arranging and polishing. First of all, you must consider the order of the four groups. Which one is the most important and where do you want it, first or last? If you decide that the "Writing" group is the most important and that "Reading" is the second in importance, you might place "Writing" last and "Reading" first. If you use these positions, will the other groups fit into place satisfactorily? Then, you have other questions to consider. What is the very best order of main points and sub-points? Should you combine some items and split others? Are there any unneeded points? If so, leave them out. Is the wording of the central idea clear and forceful? Do you have parallel form in each sequence? And, finally, what are you going to write for a strong conclusion? When you have settled these questions, you might come out with an outline like this:

CENTRAL IDEA: *To prepare for college in high school English, you should develop your language skills.*

1. *Reading*

   a. College reading assignments are long and difficult.

   b. You must *know* in an orderly way what you have to read.

    c. You should practice now with solid reading matter, like that in college textbooks.

        (1) Learn to underline.

        (2) Learn to outline for organization and to take notes.

        (3) Practice asking yourself key questions and answering them.

        (4) Practice retelling to others the content of what you have read.

2. *Speaking*

    a. Many colleges require public speaking of freshmen.

    b. You should get speaking practice now.

        (1) Gives you self-confidence.

        (2) Helps you to overcome common weaknesses in delivery.

        (3) Teaches you to prepare a well-organized talk.

3. *Listening*

    a. In college much learning comes from listening to classroom lectures.

    b. Your ability to listen effectively can be developed through practice.

        (1) Learn to remember what you hear by noting the main points and their relationships.

        (2) Learn to take good notes while listening.

4. *Writing*

    a. Freshman composition is required in many colleges.

    b. College writing standards are high.

        (1) Many fail because of poor writing.

        (2) You are expected to know spelling, punctuation, and good usage.

        (3) College writing must be accurate and clear.

    c. You should practice often, for you can learn to write only by writing.

        (1) Practice hardest on exposition, that is, explaining things.

        (2) Learn to write different kinds of paragraphs, developing your thoughts in various ways.

        (3) Learn to organize your thoughts, with a beginning, a middle, and a conclusion.

        (4) Learn to connect your sentences in thought so that they flow smoothly.

5. *Conclusion*

It is these language skills that pay off in college. Get a head start by developing them now.

Such is the way that useful outlines are made. Remember that the outline is for you alone and that it is serviceable when it enables you to:

1. Arrange your points or topics in the best order.

2. Combine in groups those things that go together.

4
WRITING A RESEARCH PAPER

One fine day your instructor may announce, "Four weeks from today you are to turn in a research paper; about a thousand words will do. Be sure to get my approval of your topic before beginning this project."

A research paper? Just what does that mean? It means an investigative paper based on information that you gather from outside sources such as books, articles, and interviews. And why does the instructor insist on approving your topic before you begin? Because you might choose a topic that is too broad, like "How to Manage Your Own Business," and the large amount of information available would be unmanageable in a short paper. Or you might choose too narrow a subject, like "The Feeding Habits of the Coral Snake," about which your library might yield only a fragment of information.

The word "research" is commonly associated with scientists and all the elaborate equipment of their laboratories. Much scientific work is indeed research, but we all use some kind of research from time to time in our everyday activities. Lawyers research their cases, architects research the physical possibilities of their designs, journalists research the events that make the news, and careful consumers research items before they buy them—automobiles, bicycles, cameras, tape decks. You may have researched several colleges before selecting one. Research, essentially, means careful investigation, or thorough study. The methods of research are valuable in school and afterward. Not all research involves the writing of a formal report, but writing of some kind is usual—if only in brief notes to oneself.

Most of the serious papers that you will write for your courses will involve some research—careful investigation—into appropriate subjects. Students often find that they learn more and have a greater sense of accomplishment in their school work as a result of having written successful research papers.

Efficiency in research begins with the mastery of procedures. Some of these procedures are so well established that they are virtually rules, but others are flexible and can be adapted to your own needs and habits.

In general, the procedure of writing a research paper consists of these steps: (1) selecting a subject; (2) finding reference materials; (3) evaluating reference materials; (4) reading relevant materials, at the same time keeping a card file of works consulted; (5) formulating a thesis, that is, your key idea; (6) taking notes; (7) arranging your material; (8) writing the paper; (9) footnoting. You will not always be performing these steps in exactly this order, and often you will be performing several of them at the same time. You will see why as we take a look at each of the steps.

Selecting a Subject

This initial step is sometimes the most troublesome, and if not taken thoughtfully can cause undesirable delays. Perhaps your instructor will have selected a subject for you. More often than not, though, an assigned subject will be too general for you to handle without some preliminary considerations. Subject assignments such as wildlife conservation or electronics or the history of architecture are invitations to you to be selective. Such general subjects are comprehensive enough to require a book-length paper—something no instructor wants from you. Therefore, your first task is to narrow or limit the subject so it can be handled in a reasonable amount of space and time.

When faced with a broad or vague subject, the best way to begin is to familiarize yourself with as many aspects of it as you can. Start searching for information; read about the subject. Soon you will find that there are a number of aspects of the subject, any one of which could be the subject of your paper. Though wildlife conservation is too broad a subject, the conservation of Montana's native flowers narrows it down to a reasonable area; the same is true of protecting grizzly bears and people from each other or saving swamps in Florida. Similarly, the history of architecture is much too broad a subject, but ancient Greek temples would be a manageable possibility. North American Colonial architecture would be another possibility, and we will use this one as a springboard in the discussion of "Formulating a Thesis."

As you read about your subject and find a possible writing topic, ask yourself questions about it. Try questions such as, "Am I able to do this?" "Do I want to know about this enough to do the work necessary?" As you progress, you will think of other appropriate questions, and they will lead you to more information. Questions such as "Who knows most about this?" "What caused it?" "What effect does it have?" "How does it compare with other things like it?" and "How does it differ from things unlike it?" will lead you to more information. Such questions will help you notice information that otherwise you might overlook. You will quickly discover that posing questions about your subject and finding reference materials about it are closely related, as are all the steps of writing such a paper.

Finding Reference Materials

If you have not already done so, you will soon learn that the most important and useful information that you acquire in your education is not raw information, such as the capital of Bulgaria, but *where* such raw information may be reliably found. Where can you find reliable information about your subject? This is a vital step in the writing of your research paper. Remember, research is *careful investigation,* and the results of your research—the written paper in this case—can be no better than the sources that you investigate.

CARD CATALOG

The largest key to information available to you is the library card catalog. You should take time to familiarize yourself with the workings of the card catalog in your library. Your librarian may be willing to help you learn to use this catalog. The card catalog is like an index to the holdings of the library. You will see that the cards are arranged alphabetically, by authors, by book titles, and by subjects. If you wish to know what books the library has on bee-keeping, look under that heading as a subject in the card catalog. There are a number of aids in the use of the catalog, such as the standard list of subjects commonly used by libraries. As with other reference materials the card catalog can, through cross-references, lead you to books and articles that would otherwise escape your attention.

ENCYCLOPEDIC WORKS

Besides the card catalog, you should look into encyclopedias, indexes, almanacs, yearbooks, atlases, dictionaries of biography, and so on. Each work can lead you further to another—try to follow up such leads as come your way. There are many encyclopedias besides the familiar *Encyclopedia Americana, Encyclopaedia Britannica, Collier's Encyclopedia,* and the *Columbia Encyclopedia.* There are specialized works such as the *Encyclopedia of World Art,* the *McGraw-Hill Encyclopedia of Science and Technology,* and the *International Encyclopedia of the Social Sciences.*

INDEXES AND ALMANACS

A very helpful index for you will be the *Readers' Guide to Periodical Literature.* This work provides information about where to find articles published in the most widely read magazines in any given year; you may look up the information by subject or by author. Other indexes that may be helpful are the *Art Index, Biography Index, Cumulative Book Index, International Index to Periodicals,* and the *New York Times Index.* Your instructor or librarian may suggest other specialized indexes. Don't overlook almanacs, such as *The World Almanac and Book of Facts,* the *Information Please Almanac,* and *The New York Times Encyclopedic Almanac;* such works are sometimes the most convenient places to find simple but obscure information, like David Janssen's place and year of birth.

In your search for information, go from the general sources, like the encyclopedias, to the more specific ones, like articles in magazines and entire books on your subject. With books, learn to use the table of contents and the index to find exactly what you are looking for.

Evaluating Reference Materials

As you find books and articles about your subject, you should begin to develop a sense of the nature and importance of the information that you discover. Not everything you read is necessarily factual. Much of it will be opinion, and opinions can vary from worthwhile to untrustworthy. You will find that some writers are specialists on certain subjects and that some writers on the same subjects are but slightly familiar with their material; that some writers are objective—that is, free from personal bias—and others are not; that some write in order to explain something and others write to persuade the reader to think or act in a certain way. It is not always easy to recognize the motives of writers or the validity of what they write, but you should make the effort.

PRIMARY AND SECONDARY SOURCES

Another problem that arises in handling source material is determining whether the material is a primary or secondary source. A primary source, generally, is an original one—a letter, a diary, an autobiography, a memoir, an interview, a speech, a document, and the like. A secondary source is something written from or about primary sources, secondhand, as it were. A letter written by Abraham Lincoln is a primary source of Lincoln's ideas on the subjects touched on in the letter. An article discussing the contents of the letter is a secondary source. You should strive to depend mostly on primary sources, if possible; otherwise, you are merely passing on the selected facts, judgments, and opinions of other writers.

Keeping a Bibliographic Card File

As you read about your subject, you should keep an accurate record of every work you consult, using one 3-by-5 card for each source. Place on each card all the bibliographical information available for the work it refers to: the author's name, the title, the place of publication, the publisher, and the date of publication. The first sample here shows the format suitable for a book. For

Hume, Ruth

Great Women of Medicine.

New york: Random House, 1964.

an article appearing in a journal, magazine, or newspaper, include not only the author's name, and the title of the article, but also the name of the periodical, its date, and the pages where the article can be found. See the second sample, opposite page.

These cards will be the basis for your bibliography or reference list of sources consulted, which appears at the end of a research paper.

Gilliatt, Penelope

"The Current Cinema." The New
Yorker, 20 September 1976,
pp. 114-118.

Formulating a Thesis

A thesis is the central idea of your paper, the main point that
your paper explains or upholds, in the form of a sentence. If you
are asked, "What is your paper about?" you should be able to incorporate your thesis in the answer, as in "My paper shows that
color is an important element in packaging and marketing." This
answer includes a thesis sentence: "Color is an important element
in packaging and marketing." It can be explained, illustrated, and
supported by proof; and it is comprehensive enough to justify a
research paper but not so sweeping as to require book-length
treatment.

Try to think about possible thesis sentences as you investigate
your subject. Suppose you have narrowed down the history of
architecture to "North American Colonial architecture," one of the
possibilities mentioned in connection with selecting a subject. This
is now your writing topic or subject. But a subject is not a thesis.
Ask yourself what you can say *about* the subject. "North American
Colonial architecture is . . ."—what? The thesis sentence must have
a verb. The verb need not be *is* or any other form of *to be,* however. Consider *declined* or *derived* as possibilities in the example
just given. These verbs could give you thesis sentences like these:
"North American Colonial architecture in public buildings began
to decline with the arrival of the Greek Revival style"; "North
American Colonial domestic architecture derived from seventeenth-
century British architecture." But forms of *to be* do produce good
thesis sentences, of course. This is an example: "North American
Colonial mansions were handsome to look at and comfortable to
live in."

You should correlate your thesis with the purpose of your paper. The sooner you can settle on a specific purpose, the sooner you will be able to frame a thesis. Is your purpose to show how something happened, to demonstrate how something works, to explain a relationship between two things or events, to uphold the truth of a proposition, to evaluate a piece of work or a movement, to clarify a process—or something else? For example, suppose your purpose is to help your reader evaluate tennis rackets so as to be able to choose the most suitable one. A thesis sentence incorporating this purpose might be: "The selection of a good tennis racket requires consideration of quality and choice of materials, weight and balance, grip, and tension and durability of the strings." At first thought this may sound like too narrow a subject, but as you gather more and more information, you will find abundant material for a 1000-word paper.

Taking Notes

While it is generally true that writers develop their own systems of taking notes in the course of research, there is no reason why the beginner should be handicapped by lack of guidance. There are rules of common sense that any efficient system of note-taking will incorporate. Once you have compiled a set of notes, you will find them much more convenient to work with while writing than the original sources themselves. Some materials cannot be removed from the library, and constantly returning to the microfilm machine can be a nuisance; anyway, you may find, when you get up steam (or when the deadline is near!), that you are writing during hours when the library is closed. For these reasons, you will want your notes to be complete enough so that you do not have to double back or leave holes to be filled in.

You will find it much easier to use note cards than to keep a running account in a notebook—it is simpler to arrange and re-arrange cards than to keep track of things among a number of bound pages. The usual cards used for this sort of work are 5 by 8 inches in size.

Since you are using cards so that you will be able to arrange and re-arrange them, it is important not to put too much information on any one card. Each card should be a note of one specific point that you have found in one source. You may or may not include some of the original language of the original author on a card.

Usually, it is better to paraphrase the original language, though some writers take down the actual words and leave the paraphrasing until later. In any case, when you do want to copy the language of the original because it is striking or worthy of quotation, be sure to use quotation marks on your note card so you won't forget later that those skilfully chosen and elegantly arranged words are not your own.

Try to avoid writing your paper on the cards. That is, don't write lengthy notes and then merely connect them together later until you have filled the required number of pages. The basic theory behind a research paper is that it consists of facts and opinions found elsewhere that you have arranged according to your own plan and connected together with your own thoughts.

> Computer science will continue to offer increasing opportunities for careers for many years to come.
>
> ---
>
> John Millar Carroll, *Careers and Opportunities in Computer Science* (New York: E. P. Dutton, 1967), p. 3.

The note cards should clearly identify the works consulted. The sample card shown here includes six items of information about the work consulted: author's name, title of book, place of publication, publisher, date of publication, and the page number showing where the specific information was found. In this case, the information is the note-taker's paraphrase of the author's general point. Since each source consulted also has its own bibliographic card and since the note cards are for your own eyes only, you can, of course, save time by abbreviating sources. "Carroll, *Careers*, p. 3" would be enough for the sample note card.

To sum up, your note cards should serve you as the raw materials of your paper, ready for use when and where you want them. They should be reminders of what you have read: so-and-so's opinion, such-and-such a fact. And they should be clear and accurate records of words you wish to quote. (They also are essential in showing where you got your information; that aspect of note cards is discussed under "Footnoting," p. 169.)

Arranging Your Material

The order in which you arrange your material is important in writing a research paper. Three of the types of arrangement most often used follow. As you will see, the nature of your thesis can, at times, almost dictate the arrangement.

1. Some papers can be best arranged by sequencing the main divisions of the material in *order of importance*. For example, a paper on pollution perils in northern Illinois might begin with the occasional light pollution of country streams by farm chemicals and end with the overwhelming pollution of the air by the factories and mills around the heavily populated Chicago area.

2. Other papers may lend themselves to a *condition-and-reasons,* or *cause-and-effect,* arrangement, as in a paper on juvenile delinquency in Valley Junction. Here you could begin by describing the current condition—vandalism, thievery, lawless driving, pill-popping by teenagers—and then go on to the probable reasons for this condition—absence of school homework, not enough recreational facilities or counseling, and so on.

3. Still other papers might be planned with a *compare-and-contrast* arrangement. In this category might be a paper with the thesis, "The present trend of collecting classic antique cars of 1920–1925 vintage is understandable." Here you would compare cars of the period in terms of their construction, performance, and beauty and contrast them with earlier and later cars.

In addition to these three kinds of arrangement, there are many others available to you. Any one that makes sense will do. Sometimes, as in the tennis-racket example cited above, you could use any order of the four divisions of the subject mentioned in the thesis sentence, provided you keep the same order in both the thesis sentence and in the body of the paper.

After you are well under way in your research, make a rough tentative outline, stating your thesis (main idea) and listing the main points and subpoints in an order you think will work. You should now consult "Organizing by Outline," pages 149–159. You may already have begun to organize your note cards in a preliminary way. Whether you have or not, this is the time to group them in order, according to your outline. Now everything will begin to mesh together. As you continue your research to fill in gaps in your knowledge, you may find that you have to change your outline. If you change your outline, you may find new items of information that are missing and have to search them out.

WRITING

Your thesis has been chosen, and you have found the best way to arrange your material. This is when you should start writing the first draft of the paper. As you write, you may have to discard material that proves to be irrelevant to the points you have listed. Also, as you write, you may realize that you still do not have enough supporting information for some of your points, and you may have to return to the library. Then revise the draft thoroughly, for first drafts normally are only a rough approximation of a final paper. As you revise, remember that the actual writing should be the best writing you can do. Clarity, word choice, sentence form, mechanics —all are just as important in a research paper as they are in any other paper.

During writing and revising, you may find that your planned arrangement doesn't work as well as you thought it would. If so, try another approach. Eventually, it should all come together in a way that seems right—a way that satisfies you.

Footnoting

Footnotes are the usual means of telling where you got your information and quotations. They are evidence that you respect your sources and that you are handling your evidence honestly. They also enable the reader to refer to the source material for further information or to check your accuracy. This does not mean that every sentence requires a footnote. For one thing, you should be writing your own ideas, at least in part, and using the source material as examples or supporting evidence. And, for another, it is not necessary to document matters of common knowledge—such as the date of Pearl Harbor Day or the states that comprised the Confederacy in the Civil War. You should begin to observe what information and ideas are commonly held and which should be clearly identified with their sources; the latter should be documented by footnotes. So also should you document the sources of direct quotations. (See **29 Quot** for details on the proper forms for direct quotations of different lengths.)

In addition to documenting sources, footnotes have another use. They are the place where the writer can offer comments or present supplementary information without encumbering the text. You will find many examples of this use in your college textbooks.

There are several methods of documenting your sources in footnotes. Here we will suggest two methods. Consult with your instructor as to which method is preferable.

The first method of footnoting is the reference-list method. A reference list is simply a numbered bibliography which is placed at the end of the paper as a basis for documenting your sources. It works this way. All the sources you have consulted are put in alphabetical order and numbered consecutively. Then, in your paper, when you wish to cite your source or refer your reader to a work, you indicate its number in parentheses at the end of your sentence and add the page number being cited. Say, for example, that you wish to refer to *Nursing as a Career* by Caroline A. Chandler and Sharon H. Kempf. Suppose that this work is number 3 in your reference list and that you wish to refer to page 152. Here is what your reference would look like: "(3: 152)." The form of the reference list will be explained in the next section entitled "Bibliography or Reference List." If your instructor prefers that you use this reference-list method, you can skip the rest of this "Footnoting" section.

But many instructors prefer the second method of footnoting, known as the traditional method. This one is more troublesome to learn, but it offers one great advantage. It will enable you to understand the footnoting of the thousands of books which have used it in the past and which use it in the present.

In the traditional method you position footnotes at the bottoms of the pages or at the end of the paper. Whichever position you choose (or whichever position your instructor prefers), standard footnote practice includes the following features:

1. Footnotes are numbered consecutively throughout the paper; each reference number is raised slightly above the text at the end of the sentence being footnoted.

2. The first line of each footnote is indented five spaces; the number is raised slightly here, also.

3. Footnotes are single-spaced, but each footnote is separated from the next by a double space.

4. In footnotes, the author's name appears in its normal order—first name first.

5. Latin words and phrases are not underlined.

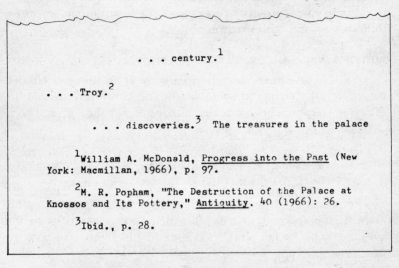

```
        . . . century.¹


  . . . Troy.²


      . . . discoveries.³  The treasures in the palace


    ¹William A. McDonald, Progress into the Past (New
York: Macmillan, 1966), p. 97.

    ²M. R. Popham, "The Destruction of the Palace at
Knossos and Its Pottery," Antiquity. 40 (1966): 26.

    ³Ibid., p. 28.
```

In the traditional method of footnoting, the form and content of the footnote are determined by the kind of source being cited. Here are some forms of footnoting that will be useful to you.

SINGLE-AUTHOR BOOK

The commonest footnote is one that cites a book by a single author. It looks like this: [1]

   [1] Leonard Koppett, *The New York Times Guide to Spectator Sports* (New York: Quadrangle Books, 1971), p. 27.

MULTIPLE-AUTHOR BOOK

At times you will use a book with more than one author.[2]

   [2] Charles Nordhoff and James Norman Hall, *Mutiny on the Bounty* (Boston: Little, Brown, 1932), pp. 125–142.

COMPILATION BY EDITOR

The same sort of format is used when referring to a book compiled by an editor.[3]

[3] Henry E. Clepper, ed., *Careers in Conservation: Opportunities in Natural Resources* (New York: Ronald Press, 1963), p. 39.

When there are more than two authors or editors for one book, it is customary in footnotes to name only the first author or editor, followed by "and others" or "et al."

AUTHOR'S WORK IN COMPILATION BY EDITOR

It is likely that when you refer to a book by an editor or editors, you will be referring to some specific author's work within it; therefore you should cite first the author and not the editor.[4]

[4] Robert Benchley, "Why Does Nobody Collect Me?" in William Targ, ed., *Carrousel for Bibliophiles: A Treasury of Tales, Narratives, Epigrams and Sundry Curious Studies Relating to a Noble Theme* (New York: Phillip C. Duschness, 1947), p. 32.

You see that the editor is not ignored completely—just put in his place. It is important to remember that you should refer to the author and his or her work first; then should follow the book in which the work appears.

AUTHOR'S WORK IN MAGAZINE, NEWSPAPER/JOURNAL

The principle just mentioned also holds true when you cite an article from a magazine.[5]

[5] Norman Cousins, "Down with Poets!" *Saturday Review of Literature,* 23 December 1944, p. 10.

[6] Elliott West, "Dirty Tricks in Denver," *The Colorado Magazine,* 52 (1975): 227.

Do you see the difference between these two footnotes? The first cites a work from a weekly periodical, and the second refers to a work from a quarterly publication. Although most publications actually have volume numbers, a publication that comes out weekly (or more frequently, as with a newspaper) is referred to only by the date of publication; however, a publication that is issued every month (or less frequently) is referred to by its volume number and year. This is done because it provides the reader with the easiest way to look up the works themselves in bound volumes in a library. Note also that when you use the volume number, you leave out the abbreviation for "page" or "pages."

Note also that in footnotes 4, 5, and 6, the titles of articles are placed in quotation marks. (See **29 Quot.**)

POEMS

Poems too are enclosed in quotation marks.[7]

[7] Archibald MacLeish, "America Was Promises," *New Republic*, 8 November 1939, p. 47.

POEM AS A BOOK

But if the poem was published as a book, you do it this way: [8]

[8] Archibald MacLeish, *America Was Promises* (New York: Duell, Sloan and Pearce, 1939), p. 5.

Book titles, play titles, motion picture titles, names of magazines, newspapers, statues, paintings, and ships are all underlined. (See **29 Quot.**) In typing and writing, underlining represents italics.

ONE VOLUME OF A SERIES

Some books appear in two or more volumes. If you wish to refer to only one of the volumes, you do it like this: [9]

[9] Theodore Roosevelt, *The Winning of the West* (New York: Putnam, 1894), III, 44.

The roman numeral is necessary to avoid confusion between the volume number and the page number.

REVISED EDITION OF BOOK

The fact that you are referring to a revised edition must be indicated because its pagination will differ from that of the previous edition. Without this information, a reader looking up your source might turn to the previous edition and fail to find your reference.[10]

[10] R. L. Oldfield, *Radio-Television and Basic Electronics*, 2nd ed. rev. (Chicago: American Technical Society, 1960), p. 85.

ENCYCLOPEDIA

When you wish to cite an article in an encyclopedia or similar reference work in which the material is arranged alphabetically, three items are all you need: the title of the article, the title of the reference work, and the date of publication.[11]

[11] "Rhetoric," *Encyclopaedia Britannica*, 1911.

INTERVIEW

When you wish to quote an expert you have interviewed, you can do it like this.[12]

[12] Otto E. Schoen-René, personal interview, Geneva, New York, 23 February 1976.

REFERENCES TO WORKS ALREADY CITED

Next, how do you make a second or third reference to a work already cited in a footnote? You don't have to write out the entire note again—there are standard ways of making subsequent references. Common Latin abbreviations are still used for this purpose. Probably the most used is "Ibid.," short for *ibidem*, meaning "in the same place." Ibid. refers to the most recent fully specified footnote. It may be repeated as long as you are continuing to refer to the same work. It is put just where other footnotes are, usually followed by a page number.[13]

[13] Ibid., p. 92.

"Op. cit." is short for *opere citato*, meaning "in the work cited." This is used with the author's name and the page number.[14]

[14] Roosevelt, op. cit., p. 49.

Such abbreviations are now used less than they used to be, but you should know them because they will appear in works that you will be using in your research.

An easier way to make subsequent references in traditional footnotes is simply to give the author's last name and the appropriate page number, like this: [15]

[15] Oldfield, p. 90.

If you have cited more than one work by the same author, then in subsequent references you should also indicate which work of his or hers you are referring to; a short version of the title is enough.[16]

[16] Clepper, *Careers in Conservation*, p. 47.

Bibliography or Reference List

A bibliography is a list of works you have consulted in the course of your research, whether or not you have referred to them or quoted from them in your paper. Your instructor may ask you to divide the bibliography into two parts, like this: include the works actually used in your paper—the works cited in the footnotes—in the first part and list all other works consulted in the second part, called "Additional Works Consulted." Some instructors prefer that a bibliography include only works actually cited in the footnotes.

A bibliography is alphabetized by author and is placed at the end of the paper. You should be able to copy your bibliographic entries from your bibliographic cards. These cards also make it easy to alphabetize your list. But be careful here, for the form of entries in a bibliography differs from the form of footnotes. So study the sample bibliography that follows as a guide to the form and punctuation of each entry. Note that this bibliography includes the works already cited in the sample footnotes.

If you have used the first method of footnoting instead of the traditional method, number the entries in your bibliography, thus transforming it into a reference list.

SAMPLE BIBLIOGRAPHY

Benchley, Robert. "Why Does Nobody Collect Me?" in *Carrousel for Bibliophiles: A Treasury of Tales, Narratives, Epigrams and Sundry Curious Studies Relating to a Noble Theme.* Ed. William Targ. New York: Phillip C. Duschness, 1947, pp. 31–35.

Carroll, John Millar. *Careers and Opportunities in Computer Science.* New York: E. P. Dutton, 1967.

Chandler, Caroline A., and Sharon H. Kempf. *Nursing as a Career.* New York: Dodd, Mead, 1970.

Clepper, Henry E., ed. *Careers in Conservation: Opportunities in Natural Resources.* New York: Ronald Press, 1963.

Corvo, Frederick B. *Hadrian the Seventh.* 1904. Rpt. New York: Dover, 1969.

Cousins, Norman. "Down with Poets!" *Saturday Review of Literature,* 23 December 1944, pp. 10–11.

Gilliatt, Penelope. "The Current Cinema." *The New Yorker,* 20 September 1976, pp. 114–118.

Hume, Ruth. *Great Women of Medicine.* New York: Random House, 1964.

Koppett, Leonard. *The New York Times Guide to Spectator Sports.* New York: Quadrangle Books, 1971.

MacLeish, Archibald. "America Was Promises." *New Republic,* 8 November 1939, pp. 46–48.

MacLeish, Archibald. *America Was Promises.* New York: Duell, Sloan and Pearce, 1939.

Nordhoff, Charles, and James Norman Hall. *Mutiny on the Bounty.* Boston: Little, Brown, 1932.

Oldfield, R. L. *Radio-Television and Basic Electronics.* 2nd ed. rev. Chicago: American Technical Society, 1960.

"Rhetoric." *Encyclopaedia Britannica.* 1911.

Roosevelt, Theodore. *The Winning of the West.* 4 vols. New York: Putnam, 1894.

Schoen-René, Otto E. Personal interview. Geneva, New York, 23 February 1976.

West, Elliott. "Dirty Tricks in Denver." *The Colorado Magazine,* 52 (1975): 225–243.

The bibliography or reference list is as important as your research has made it. It will reveal the kinds of authorities you have consulted, how recent or how timely their work was, and the kinds of places you looked into for information. A scholar who is an expert in a certain area, looking at an article in that area, often scans the bibliography first to see whether the respected authorities have been consulted by the writer; if they have not been consulted and cited, the expert may immediately suspect that the paper is of little worth. A well-done bibliography gives a writer a sense of pride and accomplishment in itself.

The Finished Paper

No matter how much trouble your research paper may have caused you, it will prove to have been a rewarding experience if done with care and patience. As you gain practice in the steps outlined here and become confident that you, yourself, can do serious investigative work, you will find the work less burdensome and increasingly enjoyable. Most important, if you have done your work well, you will have learned a good deal about your subject and you will have succeeded in communicating your findings to other people.

5
WRITING ESSAY EXAMINATIONS

In college you will have to take many essay examinations. An essay examination is one in which you answer questions in your own words. It tests not only your knowledge and understanding of the subject, but also your skill in reading and writing. It tests your skill in reading because it requires you to find out *exactly* what the questions *mean*, not approximately what they are concerned with. It tests your skill in writing because, if you are to be successful, you must make your meaning unequivocally clear, you must employ a reasonable organization with sufficient thought development, and you must make every word count. And all this you must accomplish in what is essentially a first draft. No wonder, then, that it is difficult to write a good essay examination. There are, however, a few recommended methods and procedures that you can follow to advantage in taking essay examinations, and these are presented below to show you how to cope with your college examinations.

Before the Examination

Before you attempt to write an essay examination you must have a reasonable command of the subject. Of course, you cannot be expected to know every detail, but you should have in mind an orderly view of the subject, and you should know well those parts of the subject that have received emphasis in class. These two requirements are minimum; from here on you should fill in as much as your time permits. Many students find it helpful to make out the examination that they would give if they were the instructor and then write out the answers to their own questions. Sometimes, too, students can work usefully in pairs, asking and answering questions.

They usually begin with broad overall questions and then work down to finer details. The important thing in this kind of review session is never to lose sight of the total organization, the view of the material, for this organization helps you to remember and to fit details into their proper place.

During the Examination

When the examination hour is at hand and you receive the questions, there are three things to bear in mind.

1. Read through the entire examination, both directions and questions, before you begin to write. Note whether a certain number of minutes or percentage points is allotted to each question. If so, you have a rough guide as to how much you are expected to go into detail. But if there is no time or percentage-point allotment, you will have to decide for yourself about the relative importance of each question. In either case, plan your time to complete the examination. Note also whether you are given a choice of questions to answer. If you are given a choice, choose. Do not go ahead and answer all the questions anyway, for only one answer will count, and you will merely waste valuable time on your extra answers.

2. Answer the easiest questions first. This will give you a mental warm-up, and the things you know well may suggest others that you might have overlooked if you had started cold on the hard questions. When you begin with other than the first question, leave plenty of space on your paper for the questions you will answer later, and keep the order of your answers the same as that of the questions.

3. Allow time to spend a few minutes at the end rereading your entire paper to tidy up the phrasing, check spelling and punctuation, and add any details that you may inadvertently have omitted.

Writing the Examination

When you are ready to begin writing, you will find certain procedures helpful.

1. Note carefully the **directive verb** that tells you what you should **do** in your answer. Directive verbs commonly used in examinations are: *explain, enumerate, list, name, compare, contrast, describe, summarize, outline, apply, justify, defend, account for, sketch, clarify, state, illustrate, discuss.* When your instructor uses one of

these verbs, you may be sure that he or she means exactly what the verb says. If, for example, you are asked to *enumerate* or *list* ten migratory birds that pass through Iowa, you are expected only to make a list of their names. You are not expected to chart their migrations or to describe their appearance or to classify them. If you do give this added information, it will add nothing to your examination grade and will deprive you of time that you need for other questions.

2. Outline and preplan your answer if it is to be of any length at all. For this purpose use a piece of scratch paper. This preplanning will help you to write an organized instead of a haphazard answer.

3. Stick to the question. Marshal the information you have that is directly relevant to the question and present it in an orderly way. Resist the temptation to make a sly transition to something you know well and to go out on this area of knowledge. You will not fool anybody, least of all your instructor.

4. Begin your answer with a general statement or topic sentence and develop this according to the methods of thought development you learned in the section entitled "Developing Thought in Paragraphs." This technique works well with many discussion questions, though not with all questions.

You should also be aware of the following caveats in answering examination questions:

1. Do not repeat in other words what you have already said. Suppose, for instance, that you are confronted with this question on a humanities examination: "Contrast the philosophy of the Golden Age in Greece with that of the Hellenistic period." Your answer might well begin with a general statement or topic sentence like this: "Hellenistic philosophers had generally less faith in the power of reason than the Athenian philosophers during the Golden Age." This is a good beginning which you can develop. But here is the way a thoughtless student might continue the answer: "The Hellenistic philosophers were less rational than the Golden Age philosophers. They did not think that reason could solve all of man's problems, while the philosophers of the Golden Age believed that man was capable of arriving at answers to basic problems by using his power of reason." In this answer nothing has really been added to the opening general statement; the second and third sentences merely repeat in other words what has already been said.

2. Do not digress into material that does not answer the question.

As an example let us look again at the same question: "*Contrast* the philosophy of the Golden Age in Greece with that of the Hellenistic period." A student might begin with an acceptable general statement: "The philosophers of the Golden Age in Greece had greater faith in the power of reason than those of the Hellenistic period." But suppose that the student continued by naming all the philosophers of the two periods, giving their dates and the schools to which they belonged, but not telling what they believed. Or suppose the student wrote a paragraph telling why the Hellenistic philosophers had less faith in reason, speaking of their disillusionment following the Peloponnesian Wars, the ever-present fear of Persia, the conquests of Macedonia, the economic hardships of the masses, and so on. Both of these answers would be digressions: they do not answer the question, "*Contrast the philosophy of . . .*"

3. Do not use language that is too broad and general. Here is a question that calls for specific details: "*Describe* briefly the three orders of Greek architecture." An answer in this vein would be worthless: "In Greece there were three orders of architecture. Each one had its own characteristics, its own particular style, and its own distinctive claim to beauty. The three varied considerably in many details and were modified in some degree according to the type of building in which they were employed."

4. Do not bluff. The attempt to use elegant but empty language to conceal ignorance never works, and it can be detrimental to you in two ways. First, it wastes time that you might profitably use on other questions. Second, it may irritate your instructor—and it should—because it suggests a lack of intellectual honesty.

PRACTICE EXAMINATION EXERCISE 1

This is the first of two examination exercises designed to help you learn to write better essay examinations.

Step A.   Study carefully the essay, "On Dealing with Stereotypes," that begins below and then write out the answers to the following questions, consulting the essay to make sure that your answers are as nearly perfect as you can make them.

1. *(20 points)* Define and illustrate stereotypes. (Note the two directive verbs and be sure that your answer contains both a definition and at least one illustration.)

2. *(30 points)* Discuss the harm that stereotypes can do. (Do not be deceived by the directive verb *discuss,* which seems to open wide the door to anything you wish to pour out on the subject. Actually, the essay mentions four ways in which stereotypes can do harm, and your instructor will expect you to include these four in your answer, whatever else you might wish to say.)

3. *(40 points)* Explain how we acquire stereotypes and show how some become deeply ingrained and get a real grip on us. (This is the fattest question, with 40 points, so prepare to do yourself justice here. Note that there are two parts. The answer to this question lies in different parts of the essay, and you will be expected to put these parts together in a single coherent explanation.)

4. *(10 points)* Describe, in one sentence, the two identifiable methods by which schools deal with stereotypes. (Be sure to follow the one-sentence limitation here. If you do not, you may be downgraded for slovenly reading.)

Now as you go ahead and study the essay you will observe that its organization is not as tight and lucid as you might wish. Make the best of it, keeping in mind that plenty of your college reading will be equally intractable. But the meat is there, and in your class discussion of the answers there should be no doubt about what the answers should contain for full credit.

ON DEALING WITH STEREOTYPES

Reading and discussion of books will inevitably reveal that students bring to their experiences in literature some fixed and rigid ideas about groups of people and their characteristics. Teachers need to develop programs which will help children not only to deal with these stereotypes, but also to expand their ideas about people and become more aware of the blocks which stereotyped thinking produces.

Walter Lippmann pointed out, some twenty years ago, how badly distorted our thinking often is by the false images we have of other people. Ever since, many of us have felt eager to eradicate such distortions and stereotypes from our thinking, or at least to immobilize them. . . .

Teachers need to know about stereotypes as one element in conditioning the attitudes of their students; they need to investigate the particular stereotypes which their students learn in their family and community life, and they need to plan a school program which will help their students to deal with these stereotypes as false or inadequate generalizations. Actually, stereotypes are derived from limited experience. Instead of firsthand knowledge, the general culture in which we have grown up has provided us with capsule interpretations of people's motives and behavior which most of us have been naïve enough to swallow whole.

As a matter of fact, most of us do not know how ignorant we are of people who live in the same community who belong to different economic, religious, social, or racial groups from ours. We have gathered impressions of them since early childhood from seeing them around or from very limited contacts, and these impressions have often become set mental images—"pictures in your head," as Walter Lippmann would say. Only too easily these snap judgments have been suggested by our associates, friends, and family members in the first place and then reinforced by popular fiction, advertisements, cartoons, stage jokes, hearsay, and the like. Thus, we sometimes have quite clear images of the "lazy Mexicans," "shanty Irish," dumb Negroes," "scheming Jews," or "sly Japs," although we may have had few, if any, occasions to know individuals from these groups as fellow human beings.

It is these set impressions or pictures-in-your-head that are usually called "stereotypes." In one way or another, they enter into very nearly all our thinking and are applied to many persons with whom we are not in daily, intimate contact. Most of us are aware of such stereotypes because we have found ourselves at one time or another circumscribed or categorized by them. What teacher has not been greeted by child or parent with the remark, "But you don't act like a teacher!" What teacher has not at one time or another been forced by community pressure to dress or entertain or talk like a schoolmarm? We probably also know the popular assumptions about social workers, policemen, lawyers, and workers—especially if they belong to a union. We are familiar with the notions that the rich are usually idle or dissolute, and that the younger generation is still bent on going to the dogs as it is believed to have been doing ever since the world began.

There might not be any very serious harm in snap judgments and false pictures of this kind were it not that they can come between us and reality. For example, consider the country "hick" who has so often amused us in the movies and the funnies. When rural people have come to live in urban centers, they have sometimes found their neighbors reacting to them in terms of their reputation as "hillbillies" or "greenhorns." The story is told of certain New York students, who volunteered to help harvest the crops during the wartime shortage of manpower, that for weeks they could not adjust to the necessity of learning from farmers how to do things. They could not make connections with rural life because of their assumptions that all country folk were uncouth, dull, unskilled, unsophisticated, and behind the times. Some of the country people may have been led astray quite as much by their fear that all city people are "slick."

It is important to emphasize that these false pictures and distortions often contain some element of truth. Stereotypes would not be half as misleading as they are if they did not carry a measure of conviction because of something definitely recognizable about them. They are to the mind precisely what cartoon caricatures are to the eye. Stereotypes may accordingly be said to derive from the all but universal habit of quick generalization from inadequate information. We quite naturally prefer slogans and "ten easy lessons" to reasoned analysis, and we try to write so that "he who runs may read." From the educational viewpoint the dependence upon stereotypes and other pattern thinking amounts to virtual abandonment of man's best gift for shaping his life—the power really to use his mind. Furthermore, dependence upon stereotypes prevents the development of the habit of constantly reexamining our generalizations about people. Even if the consequences for human relations were not so apparent and harmful, we would still need to develop ability to interpret new situations in terms of their potentialities instead of accepting stereotypes. Education is obligated to address itself to this task of constantly revising our interpretations and analyses.

But stereotypes can have a more damaging effect. Sometimes the stereotype grew out of a trait or situation that prevailed in the past but which is now undergoing change. The distortion may reflect what one group wants to believe about the other in order to justify its own traditional place in society. Thus, Uncle Tom or the mammy in *Gone with the Wind* may be fairly accurate historical portraits. They become hated symbols only when the dominant culture insists that they represent "the Negro's proper place," or when they are cited as evidence of the "benevolence" of slavery in the Old South. Stereotypes of this category not only reflect limited experience, but also they are used in defense of discrimination. Such stereotypes are the false images about which we are most likely to be unreasonable and defensive, especially when the suspicion may have arisen in our own minds that perhaps they are not as fair and true as we wish they were.

Pictures-in-the-head which have these emotional connotations usually get their real grip on us during childhood training. From infancy we are taught our "appropriate" social roles, as well as the manners, conduct, and dress that are suitable for people like us. Parents frequently compare or contrast the behavior they advocate with that typically associated with other people in the population whose standing is known to be undesirable. The little girl who wants a cerise sweater may be told, "But that is Indian pink; do you want to look like the old squaw we saw in the mountains last summer?" Other children may be admonished not to "act harum-scarum in Sunday school like little wild Indians," or to take a bath so that "teacher will not think you come from a Dago family!" Such parents are teaching their children more than good taste in dress, good manners in church, or cleanliness. The tone of voice, the particular words chosen, clearly indicate that the children from the groups used as bad examples are not wanted around. Stereotypes acquired in this fashion are often so deeply ingrained that most of us are not conscious of how or when we first got them. Any question or challenge of them is, accordingly, like digging into basic assumptions and the very foundations of life.

Lillian Smith has given us a classic description of the way learning about people in subservient roles takes place in the family.

It is not easy to pick up such a life and pull out of it those strands that have to do with color, with Negro-white relationships, for they are knit of the same fibers that have gone into the making of the whole fabric; they are woven into its most basic patterns and designs. The mother who taught me what I know of tenderness and love and compassion taught me also the bleak rituals of keeping the Negro in his place. The father who rebuked me for an air of superiority toward schoolmates from the mill settlement, and rounded out his rebuke by gravely reminding me that "all men are brothers," also taught me the steel-like inhuman decorums I must demand of every colored male.

Neither the Negro nor sex was often discussed in my home. We were given little formal instruction in these difficult matters, but we learned our lessons well. We learned the intricate system of taboos, of renunciations and compensations of manners, voice modulations, words, along with our prayers, our toilet habits, and our games. I do not remember how or when, but I know that by the time I had learned that God is love, that Jesus is His Son, that all men are brothers with a common Father, I also knew that I was better than a Negro, that all black folk have their place and must be kept in it, and that a terrifying disaster would befall the South if ever I treated a Negro as my social equal.

"Growing into Freedom," *Common Ground,* 4 (Autumn 1943), 47–52

While teachers do not need to know the whole technical analysis concerning stereotypes, their recognition of these points will be helpful in planning a class or school program: that stereotypes exist in our culture; that they enter into nearly all of our thinking; that they are rigid, emotionally reinforced generalizations not easily revised in the light of new experience and information; that they come between us and reality; that they contain some element of truth; that they may represent holdovers from the past or are rationalizations of the wishes of people; that they are learned and underlined in the family and other group situations where status, affection, and understanding of role are important determinants of their feeling content. School programs will more successfully undermine those stereotypes which are produced by limited experience and inadequate ways of thinking—in short, those that are verbalizations without support from social pressures. Such programs will need to attack more vigorously and with more thought-out strategy those stereotypes which are reinforced by patterns of community status, practices of discrimination, and social prejudice. The degree to which these stereotypes yield to treatment in school depends on a good many factors outside the teachers' control.

There are two identifiable methods of dealing with stereotypes. Some schools have taken from their shelves, or refused to purchase, books containing those false images which are a source of particular objection and grievance to some minority groups. Other schools have built units of study and reading around the positive contributions to American life of different ethnic strains. It will be worth while to examine both of these methods in some detail.

Literature for Human Understanding
(Washington: American Council on Education, 1948;
adapted by permission from pp. 13–18)

Step B.   Following are four series of answers that college-freshmen have given to the same four questions. Study these answers and give each one the number of points that you think it deserves. In each case where you give less than full credit, be able to justify your grading; that is, be able to point out just where and how the writer of the answer went wrong, considering especially what you have learned in "Writing Essay Examinations."

1. *(20 points)* Define and illustrate stereotypes.

ANSWERS (1)

1. Stereotypes are rigid, emotionally reinforced generalizations about groups of people and are derived from lack of experience. An example of a stereotype is the notion that all Mexicans are lazy. Another example is the generalization that all Jews are overly money conscious.

2. Stereotypes are fixed and rigid ideas concerning certain groups of people and their characteristics. An illustration of this is the fixed idea that whites are much better and in a higher class than blacks. They consider themselves better in every respect.

3. A stereotype, by the author of the pamphlet, is one who has a set picture in his mind about certain things in general or one thing in particular. A stereotype usually knows little about the subject, but has heard an opinion from an acquaintance or friend. The lack of knowledge is usually the main cause for a stereotype to develop.

4. Stereotypes are very common, and all people are likely to have them. Some common stereotypes are "lazy Mexicans," "shanty Irish," "scheming Japs," and "dumb Negroes." It is probably safe to say that there is no one who does not possess a good many of such stereotypes.

5. Stereotypes are "mind pictures." They are ideas that people get about another group of people or things. The majority of these stereotypes are not true. There is just enough suggestion of truth that people tend to believe the whole thing rather than separating the "fact from fiction." Here are some illustrations of stereotypes: (1) The Jew who is "stingy," getting

every cent's worth and maybe cheating a little bit. (2) The dumb, dirty Negro. (3) The old maid schoolteacher who is expected to dress in black, wear her hair in a bun, spend her nights reading and associating only with other old maids. (4) The kids from the poorer section of town who are always classed as "juvenile delinquents." (5) The rich people who are always complete snobs and never do anything worthwhile. (6) The "absent-minded professor."

I could go on enumerating the common stereotypes but they would all prove the same point. That point is that very few people are actually like the stereotype they are supposed to be and even the ones that are a little bit are not enough in number to support such a stereotype.

2. *(30 points)* **Discuss the harm that stereotypes can do.**

ANSWERS (2)

1. Stereotypes can cause the loss of the greatest power of our minds, that of thinking. If a person has let stereotypes take over in his mind, it will function thus: "This" is true because I learned it as a child. "That" is true because Jim Jones said so. Therefore I need not think since I know everything anyway.

Stereotypes can cause us to stop changing our generalities. Once we have let stereotypes take over we no longer change our minds.

Stereotypes can come between us and reality. For instance, we are brought up on the farm with the idea that all city people are "slickers" and none of them can be trusted. If we then are in the city, we will think that all city folks are bad even if some have more goodness in them than do some rural folks.

2. Stereotypes are harmful because they come between man and reality. They rob him of his power to think and reason. Also, stereotypes may serve to defend and protect practices which are not entirely good for, or beneficial to, mankind as a whole.

3. Stereotypes can be very harmful in that they often give false ideas and conceptions of certain things. An example of this would be to say: "White people are superior to dark people." This is not true and leads you to believe that those with dark skins are less intelligent than those with lighter skins. An example of how this misconception could be harmful might be seen in this way.

Suppose you were an employer and you were interviewing applicants for a certain job. The applicants have been eliminated until there are only two left, one with light skin and one with dark. The person with the dark skin may have more training in the specific job and therefore be more suited for the position than the lighter-skinned person. But the job is one of prestige, and because of the belief in the stereotype that the whites are more intelligent than darks, you place the light-skinned person in the position instead of the dark, even though the dark-skinned person is better qualified.

This is just one example of how a stereotype can be harmful. Stereotypes lead us to believe things about people that are not true. By believing these things we judge accordingly, and our judgment of a person can often be false because of the stereotype.

4. Stereotypes harm religious, political, racial, and social groups both locally and nationally. They can cause bad feelings between friends, towns, or even nations. People have been known to kill because they had been taught that the victim was useful to no one and should therefore be disposed of. A feeling or belief toward a person or thing can harm an individual emotionally. For instance, a person may be pushed to the point of a nervous breakdown because, contrary to his childhood teachings, he likes a group of people, for example, Negroes or Jews. It may prey on his mind that he is abnormal or something. Stereotypes harm us mentally because they stop the healthy, normal process of thinking for ourselves. We hear something and instead of investigating we simply accept it and continue on.

5. Because stereotypes are not wholly truthful, some people get false impressions about other people or things. This is very harmful because a person might have nothing to do with someone whom he thinks he is superior to. A false impression like this could even go so far as to build up hate in the man. It could also make the person lose many friends and acquaintances.

3. *(40 points)* Explain how we acquire stereotypes and show how some become deeply ingrained and get a real grip on us.

ANSWERS (3)

1. Most of us acquire our use of stereotypes quite young from our parents, relatives, and so on. Then, as we grow older, we become influenced by such things as motion pictures, advertisements, and books. Our friends also have a big part in influencing us. After continual use of these false images they become an actual part of our thinking.

2. We acquire most of our stereotypes during childhood. Our folks may often try to get us to become better socially by telling us not to be like the dirty Mexicans, or not to dress gaudy like the blacks. All of these are generalizations that are acquired from lack of knowledge, experience, and understanding. When we go shopping, our mother might tell us not to go *there* because they are Jews. In some communities that are mostly Protestant, Catholics might be called "fish eaters," and this forms a stereotype in the children's minds.

The stereotypes that really get a grip on us are the ones that are evident in all institutions in our particular community. The ones that are just generalizations taken out of a book are not as hard to correct and control. In my community everyone formed stereotypes of Bahamans and Mexicans. The reason we were taught that these people were bad, lazy, and dirty was because every summer some would be shipped into our town to do detasseling. Naturally these were the worst ones. We were told not to talk to them and to stay in the house. Anyone who would talk to these detasselers would be gossipped about. This led many children in our community to think of *all* Mexicans and Bahamans as *bad*. This is deeply imprinted in our lives because we can think back and remember the incidences of the detasselers. The inferiority of the Mexicans and Bahamans was very evident in our school, family, and other organizations.

3. Everyone acquires stereotypes as he goes through life. Usually they are about people with whom he has had little experience. For instance, the man who has had little education may have the stereotype of the old-maid schoolteacher with a black dress, high shoes, and a cross disposition. The person who has never been in the military service will probably have a stereotype of a big, burly, tough army master sergeant who speaks foul language. The city boy who has always lived in the city may have the "red neck" or "hick" stereotype. When such stereotypes become deeply ingrained, they are dangerous to us because they come between us and reality, they keep us from seeing people as they really are.

4. Stereotypes are acquired most often in the pattern-forming childhood years. At an early age children accept readily what their parents and others may tell them or imply by certain remarks.

Thus, when a mother tells her children to wash well or the schoolteacher will think you come from a Dago family, the children get the idea that Dago children are not desirable. Inferences such as these are repeated and stressed more and more as the children get older and become a part of the way they think. Social pressures are brought to bear on people who do not accept a stereotype that the community believes. For example, a white man who hires a black for a top office job might face expulsion from the groups he has associated with all his life and possibly threats to the well-being of his family or person. After seeing these pressures brought against others by all his friends, a person can only feel that the stereotype must be true. No matter how much new experience or information is acquired concerning the stereotype, the person will still believe what has become ingrained in his mind all through his life.

5. Stereotypes are acquired in many ways but most often they are implanted on our minds by our parents, relatives, or close friends. Sometimes we acquire stereotypes through association with someone of this sort, and we have the same feeling toward all those who are like him.

Stereotypes become deeply ingrained and get a real grip on us because we see them almost every day in advertisements, comic strips, and magazines; or we hear them from various sources such as parents, radio, or television. After we hear and see these stereotypes so often, we feel that all people of that nationality, race, religion, or vicinity must be the same. Again, whites' attitude toward blacks is a good example. Some whites have been raised on the idea that all blacks are ignorant and militant.

4. *(10 points)* Describe, in one sentence, the two identifiable methods by which schools deal with stereotypes.

ANSWERS (4)

1. It is very necessary that schools deal with stereotypes by identifiable methods because our country has many minority groups, and these will suffer if people think of them in stereotypes. For example, if we hold in our minds the stereotypes of the "crafty Jew," the "vicious Negro," the "dirty Indian," then when we meet an honest Jew or a gentle Negro or a clean Indian, we shall misjudge them. And the school is the best place to eradicate such undesirable stereotypes because the school gets children young and can implant the right ideas early so they have a chance to grow.

2. Schools may try to combat stereotypes by keeping from the children such books or pictures that might help to develop stereotyped images, and by giving children a full and true picture of the customs, background, and contributions of groups who are usually victims of stereotypes.

3. Stereotypes are dealt with by exposing children as early as possible to books and other examples of the assets, contributions, and admirable qualities of a stereotyped person or group.

Stereotypes are also dealt with by the removal of all books or other sources of information that tend to increase or intensify the ideas concerning stereotyped people or groups.

4. Some schools do not buy books that may cause prejudice among certain groups; others build a field of study around unethical beliefs.

5. Two methods by which schools deal with stereotypes are: first, usage and discussion of material concerning stereotypes; second, avoiding stereotypes as much as possible.

PRACTICE EXAMINATION EXERCISE 2

Tomorrow you will take a half-hour practice examination on the selection below. In preparation you are asked to do the following. First, study the material carefully, underlining and marking it to help you locate the central ideas and main facts. Then, write out five precisely worded questions, the answers to which will represent the meat of the selection, and be prepared to answer your own questions. The examination will consist of five questions which your instructor believes will test your knowledge and understanding of the material; and if you take pains to apply your intelligence, you should be able to anticipate most of them. Before the examination you are to hand in your questions. After the examination you will have an opportunity to reexamine and discuss the selection and to analyze your answers.

The selection is taken from a college textbook for freshman courses in the humanities. A single day's assignment will often be five times as long. This selection, in contrast with the one on stereotypes, is neatly and lucidly organized, as many of your basic textbooks will be.

ATHENIAN LIFE IN THE GOLDEN AGE

The population of Athens in the fifth and fourth centuries was divided into three distinct groups: the citizens, the metics, and the slaves. The citizens, who numbered at the most about 160,000, included only those born of citizen parents, except for the few who were occasionally enfranchised by special law. The metics, who probably did not exceed a total of 100,000, were resident aliens, chiefly non-Athenian Greeks, although some were Phoenicians and Jews. Save for the fact that they had no political privileges and generally were not permitted to own land, the metics had equal opportunities with citizens. They could engage in any occupation they desired and participate in any social or intellectual activities. Contrary to a popular tradition, the slaves in Athens were never a majority of the population. Their maximum number does not seem to have exceeded 140,000. On the whole, they were very well treated and were often rewarded for faithful service by being set free. They could work for wages and own property, and some of them held responsible positions as minor public officials and as managers of banks.

Life in Athens stands out in rather sharp contrast to that in most other civilizations. One of its leading features was the amazing degree of social and economic equality which prevailed among all the inhabitants. Although there were many who were poor, there were few who were very rich. The average wage was the same for practically all classes of workers, skilled and unskilled alike. Nearly everyone, whether citizen, metic, or slave, ate the same kind of food, wore the same kind of clothing, and participated in the same kind of amusement. This substantial equality was enforced in part by the system of liturgies, which were services to the state rendered by wealthy men, chiefly in the form of contributions to support the drama, equip the navy, or provide for the poor.

A second outstanding characteristic of Athenian life was its poverty in comforts and luxuries. Part of this was due to the low income of the mass of the people. Teachers, sculptors, masons, carpenters, and common laborers all received the same standard wage of one drachma (about 30 cents) per day. Part of it may have been due also to the mild climate, which made possible a life of simplicity. But whatever the cause, the fact remains that, in comparison with modern standards, the Athenians endured an exceedingly impoverished existence. They knew nothing of such common things as watches, soap, newspapers, cotton cloth, sugar, tea, or coffee. Their beds had no springs, their houses had no drains, and their food consisted chiefly of barley cakes, onions, and fish, washed down with diluted wine. From the standpoint of clothing they were no better off. A rectangular piece of cloth wrapped around the body and fastened with pins at the shoulders and with a rope around the waist served as the main garment. A larger piece was draped around the body as an extra garment for outdoor wear. No one wore either stockings or socks, and few had any footgear except sandals.

But lack of comforts and luxuries was a matter of little consequence to the Athenian citizen. He was totally unable to regard these as the most important things in life. His aim was to live as interestingly and contentedly as possible without spending all his days in grinding toil for the sake of a little more comfort for his family. Nor was he interested in piling up riches as a source of power or prestige. What each citizen really wanted was a small farm or business which would provide him with a reasonable income and at the same time allow him an abundance of leisure for politics, for gossip in the marketplace, and for intellectual or artistic activities if he had the talent to enjoy them.

It is frequently supposed that the Athenian was too lazy or too snobbish to work hard for luxury and security. But such was not quite the case. It is true that there were some occupations in which he would not engage, because he considered them degrading or destructive of moral freedom. He would not break his back digging silver or copper out of a mine; such work was fit only for slaves of the lowest intellectual level. On the other hand, there is plenty of evidence to show that the great majority of Athenian citizens did not look with disdain upon manual labor. Most of them worked on their farms or in their shops as independent craftsmen. Hundreds of others earned their living as hired laborers employed either by the state or by their fellow Athenians. Cases are on record of citizens, metics, and slaves working side by side, all for the same wage, in the construction of public buildings; and in at least one instance the foreman of the crew was a slave.

In spite of expansion of trade and increase in population, the economic organization of Athenian society remained comparatively simple. Agriculture and commerce were by far the most important enterprises. Even in Pericles' day the majority of the citizens still lived in the country. Industry was not highly developed. Very few examples of large-scale production are on record, and those chiefly in the manufacture of pottery and implements of war. The largest establishment that ever existed was apparently a shield factory owned by a metic and employing 120 slaves. There was no other more than half as large. The enterprises which absorbed the most labor were the mines, but they were owned by the state and were leased in sections to petty contractors to be worked by slaves. The bulk of industry was carried on in small shops owned by individual craftsmen who produced their wares directly to the order of the consumer.

Religion underwent some notable changes in the Golden Age. The primitive polytheism and anthropomorphism of the Homeric myths were largely supplanted, among intellectuals at least, by a belief in one God as the creator and sustainer of the moral law. Such a doctrine was taught by many of the philosophers, by the poet Pindar, and by the dramatists Aeschylus and Sophocles. Other significant consequences flowed from the mystery cults. These new forms of religion first became popular in the sixth century because of the craving for an emotional faith to make up for the disappointments of life. The more important of them was the Orphic cult, which revolved around the myth of the death and resurrection of Dionysus. The other, the Eleusinian cult, had as its central theme the abduction of Persephone by Pluto, god of the nether world, and her ultimate redemption by Demeter, the great Earth Mother. Both of these cults had as their original purpose the promotion of the life-giving powers of nature, but in time they came to be fraught with a much deeper significance. They expressed to their followers the ideas of vicarious atonement, salvation in an afterlife, and ecstatic union with the divine. Although entirely inconsistent with the spirit of the ancient religion, they made a powerful appeal to certain classes of Greeks and were vary largely responsible for the spread of the belief in personal immortality. The majority of the people, however, seem to have persisted in their adherence to the worldly, optimistic, and mechanical faith of their ancestors and to have shown little concern about a conviction of sin or a desire for salvation in a life to come.

It remains to consider briefly the position of the family in Athens in the fifth and fourth centuries. Though marriage was still an important institution for the procreation of children who would become citizens of the state, there is reason to believe that family life had declined. Men of the more prosperous classes, at least, now spent the greater part of their time away from their families. Wives were relegated to an inferior position and required to remain secluded in their homes. Their place as social and intellectual companions for their husbands was taken by alien women, the famous hetaerae, many of whom were highly cultured natives of the Ionian cities. Marriage itself assumed the character of a political and economic arrangement, devoid of romantic elements. Men married wives so as to insure that at least some of their children would be legitimate and in order to obtain property in the form of a dowry. It was important also, of course, to have someone to care for the household. But husbands did not consider their wives as their equals and did not appear in public with them or encourage their participation in any form of social or intellectual activity.

6
WRITING FOR A JOB

In seeking employment, you will find two forms of writing especially useful—the resume and the letter of application which is always sent with the resume.

The Resume

The resume (pronounced *rez-uh-may*) is a summary of the basic facts that prospective employers may want to know. It is arranged so that they can read it quickly and easily and can find at a glance those items that particularly interest them. It should be carefully typed. Let us run through the form of a typical resume, step by step (though the one you devise could be different).

Your name and address should always be at the beginning:

Name _____

Address _____
                              (number and street)

_____
          (city)   (state)   (zip)

Phone _____ Best hours to call _____
          (area)   (local)

PERSONAL INFORMATION

Date of birth _____ Sex _____

Race _____ Religious preference _____

Marital status _____ No. dependents _____

Health _____ Physical disabilities _____

There are laws that forbid employers from requiring you to reveal most of this personal information, but you are free to offer any or all of this information, and it will sometimes be to your advantage to do so. An employer, for example, might have a special need for a woman or a black or a Catholic or a single man. If you meet this need, the resume will show it, and you will get preferential treatment. If you do not meet this need and therefore would not be considered, then you will save time that would otherwise be wasted in further correspondence and in interviewing. Do not be afraid to mention disabilities, even minor ones; for example, "I have a slight stutter, but it has not handicapped me in school or work" or "I wear glasses for reading and close work." The mention of such slight disabilities fosters an impression of honesty. You may, of course, omit any item of personal information that might work against you in applying for a specific job.

EDUCATION

Here you name the high school from which you graduated and the year. If you were high in scholastic achievement in your graduating class, you can give the figure; for example, "In grade-point average I was 17th from the top in a class of ninety-five." If you were in the bottom half, just skip it.

Indicate how far you have progressed in college and when you expect to receive a degree (and which degree). If you have already received a degree, of course indicate that. If it seems appropriate, indicate your areas of interest or your major field at college and any special courses you may have taken (or are taking) which might relate to the specific job. For example, if you are applying for an office job, such courses as accounting or other business courses or writing courses would be good to list. Or if you are applying for a camp job or other position that involves supervising children, any guidance or counseling courses you have taken should be listed.

Honors Received.   Use this heading to list such honors as class president, captain of basketball team, valedictorian, college dean's list, member of state championship debate team, winner of state music contest (flute), editor of school paper, recipient of college drama scholarship. Make it a subheading under your description of your high school or college education, or both. Of course if you are just a regular student, like most—if you have done your work faithfully but have not yet attained such distinctions, then simply do not include "Honors Received" in your resume.

FAVORITE ACTIVITIES (OR HOBBIES)

This is more important than you might suspect, for possible employers will make inferences about you from what you include here. For example, if you list activities like duck-hunting, skiing, canoeing, backpacking, rappelling, they are likely to infer that you are the vigorous, outdoor type who would be good at an outdoor job requiring muscular coordination and endurance. But if you list activities like stamp-collecting, chess-playing, and repairing old clocks, they might infer that you are the indoor type who would be of best service at a desk job requiring attention to detail. And if you list dancing, public speaking, committee work, collecting for charities, they could conclude that you might make a good salesman or saleswoman.

So, from all the activities that you engage in, use those that will lead your prospective employer to make the inferences that are advantageous to you.

RELEVANT EXPERIENCE

This means the experiences, at work or play, that relate to the job for which you are applying. If, for instance, you want the job of counselor in a summer camp, experiences like these would be relevant:

1. "I was a Boy Scout (or Girl Scout) for four years and won merit badges in woodsmanship, water sports, weaving, and knotting."
2. "I received my Red Cross certificate for life-saving last summer."
3. "I play tennis, volleyball, and field hockey quite well and am confident that I could coach or supervise these sports. My golf, however, is poor, and I do not feel ready to handle this sport." (This kind of negative remark is very helpful in an application: it adds credibility to your other statements.)

If you have already held two or more relevant paying jobs, it might be good to list them, with the dates you held them. Usually, you begin such a list with the most recent (or present) job and list the others in reverse chronological order.

REFERENCES

Here you list the names, addresses, and phone numbers of several people who know you well and can testify in your favor. These should be such persons as a teacher, principal, advisor, pastor, or other respected member of your community or college. If appropriate, include the name of a former employer. Be sure to ask permission of each person before using his or her name and, as a courtesy, furnish each with an addressed and stamped envelope.

EXERCISE 1

Devise a resume for one of the following jobs or for one of your choice.

1. Receptionist in a dentist's office
2. Flag girl on a construction crew (summer job)
3. Delivery man (by truck) for a nursery
4. Typist in a college office (part-time)
5. Waitress in a fashionable cocktail lounge (9 to 12 P.M.)
6. Short-order cook in a hamburger shop
7. Counselor in a camp for overweight boys (or girls)
8. Salesman in a camera shop
9. Saleswoman in a dress shop
10. Door-to-door saleswoman for a cosmetics firm

The Letter of Application

Writing a letter of application for a job is a delicate and difficult task.

The form of the letter can be any of the numerous acceptable forms of a standard business letter. The sample shown on the facing page is one that will serve your purpose.

In writing the letter, you will find it helpful to keep in mind these four suggestions:

1. The opening sentence is especially hard. Here are a few sample openings:

1. "Kindly consider me an applicant for the position of . . ."
2. "I am deeply interested in the position you advertised in the *Daily News* of October 13."
3. "This is my application for the position of night custodian as described on the college bookstore bulletin board."
4. "The Director of Employment of Gladbrook Community College has informed me that you have an opening for an experienced typist, and I should like to be considered for this job."
5. "This letter is to inquire whether you will need an additional salesman in your men's clothing department during the Christmas holidays. If such is the case, I hope you will consider me for the job."

2. Your letter should make a favorable impression. So don't overload it with the magnitude of your accomplishments, but be straightforward and reasonably modest. Also, be careful about your

510 Pine Street
Wanamingo, Minnesota 55983
November 5, 1977

Mr. Edward Parker
2415 Third Street
Rutland, Vermont 05701

Dear Mr. Parker:

My friend Jim McCleod, who worked for you during three summers, has told me that you might have an opening for a water-safety counselor in your Camp Minnesaka next summer. If such an opening occurs, I would like to be considered for the position. The enclosed resume will give you a brief summary of my qualifications.

[Here you can expand on the qualifications mentioned in the resume]

If you would like further details, I will be glad to furnish them by letter or phone.

Respectfully yours,

John Norman
John Norman

language, especially spelling. With some employers a single misspelled word can reduce your chance of success.

3. Your letter should expand on those facts in your resume that are most applicable to the particular job. Suppose, for example, that you are a young woman applying for a late afternoon job, three to six, in a household where the wife works in an office. The job requires you to meet the children after school, take care of them, and prepare the evening meal. Your resume lists cooking and baby-sitting among your favorite activities. Here your letter can expand on the facts in your resume by pointing out that you belong to a large family and have frequently taken care of your younger brothers and sisters, that you have taken two years of home economics in high school, and that you have helped your mother cook since you were in junior high school.

4. Unless your handwriting is exceptionally good, type the letter, neatly and correctly.

At this point, the most profitable next step is for you to practice writing a letter of application and to learn from the criticism of your instructor. And if your instructor is able to project or duplicate some of the most instructive letters of members of your class, you will also gain in skill and knowledge by studying their strong and weak parts.

EXERCISE 2

Write a letter of application to go with the resume you made out in Exercise 1.

Appendix
PARTS OF SPEECH

In discussing problems of writing, it is sometimes useful to know the parts of speech. So here is a succinct summary of the nine parts of speech that are mentioned in the preceding pages. Some minor or unneeded parts of speech are omitted.

Nouns are words like those in the list below.

A noun is commonly the name of something. In form, a noun normally undergoes a change for the plural, usually with the addition of *-s* or *-es* in writing, as in *books* and *churches*.

ILLUSTRATIVE LIST OF NOUNS

1. With *-s* plural — novel, student, achievement, worker, decision, idealist, deception, painting, paper, dog
2. With *-es* plural — ditch, wretch, pouch, tomato, potato
3. With other plurals — man, mouse, foot, woman, child, knife
4. With no plural — information, steam, advice, justice
5. With same singular and plural — deer, hose (= stocking), series, means
6. With foreign plurals — analysis, alumna, criterion, datum, thesis (For foreign plurals, see pp. 103–104.)

Verbs are words like those in the list below.

Many verbs show that someone or something did something; that is, they are action words, as in "Hank *hit* a homer" and "The hurricane *blew* through the town." But in some, no action is evident, as in "She *knew* her lesson," "It *seemed* difficult," and "He *looked* unhappy." Thus it is easier to identify verbs by their changes in form than by their meaning.

Verbs nearly always change form to show that the time something happened was in the past, as in *dream/dreamed* or *dreamt; breathe/breathed; ride/rode; come/came; know/knew*. They have an *-ing* form, as in *sweeping* (called the present participle) and an *-en/-ed/-t* form, as in "He was *beaten/defeated/taught*" (called the past participle).

ILLUSTRATIVE LIST OF VERBS

1. With suffixes *ed/-d/-t* for past time — credit, curse, kneel, estimate, fume, bend, imitate, lean, oblige, consider, penalize, report,

> seem, believe, toughen, wave, work, remain, cook, rule, start, look, smell

2. With vowel change to show past time — bite, blow, freeze, sting, swim, win, spring, begin, feed, catch, get, drink, hold, stand, swear, write, shake, shrink

Adjectives are words like those in the list below.

Adjectives modify nouns and pronouns, as in "a *smart* girl" and "She is *intelligent*." In form, some adjectives take the suffixes *-er* and *-est,* as in *smarter* and *smartest.* Others express these meanings of comparison by a preceding word—*more, most, less, least,* as in "more (less) intelligent" and "most (least) intelligent."

ILLUSTRATIVE LIST OF ADJECTIVES

1. With *-er/-est* forms — big, small, high, low, strong, weak, swift, nice, slow, tiny, holy, sunny

2. With preceding *more, most, less, least* — enormous, insignificant, muscular, fragile, rapid, preferable, fortunate, poetic, pompous, sensible, meddlesome, helpful, pleasant

3. With irregular forms of comparison — good, bad, far, many, well (= not sick)

4. With no comparing forms — manual, dental, lunar, tidal, natal, eternal, eventual, federal, solar, atomic, present, daily

Adverbs are words like those in the list below.

Adverbs modify (1) verbs, as in "He pleaded *eagerly*"; (2) whole sentences, as in "*Luckily,* no one was injured"; (3) adjectives, as in "He was *enormously* fat"; and occasionally adverbs, as in "She spoke *unusually* rapidly." In form, the most frequent adverb suffix is *-ly* added to an adjective, as in *pleasantly.* Some adverbs have the same form as the corresponding adjective. For example, we may say "Go slow" as well as "Go slowly" and "Come quick" as well as "Come quickly."

ILLUSTRATIVE LIST OF ADVERBS

1. With *-ly* suffix — strongly, weakly, enormously, fortunately, preferably, helplessly, merrily, swiftly

2. With no suffix — slow, quick, hard, fast, loud, here, again, tomorrow, late, well (= capably) (Bear in mind that the words in this group are adverbs only when they modify a verb, sentence, adjective, or adverb.)

The four parts of speech described above are *open classes;* that is, they accept new words into their membership, the class of nouns being the most hospitable.

In contrast to these open classes, there are five *closed classes* that we shall now examine. Each of these has a very small membership and does not accept newcomers.

Coordinating conjunctions are these eight words: *and, but, yet, for, nor, not, or, so.* Their use is to connect grammatical equivalents, such as two nouns (the union *and* the library), two adjectives (handsome *but* dumb), two participial phrases (listening intently *yet* not understanding a word), and so on. All of the coordinating conjunctions except *not* can occur between two sentences, changing them into one sentence.

Henry went to the library *but* Grace stayed in her room to study.

Jane raced to the tennis court after class, *for* the afternoon was sunny and windless.

In writing, a sentence may begin with a coordinating conjunction, especially with *and, but, or, so,* and *yet.* Here is a case in point:

Jim did not care to spend his entire Christmas vacation in study. *Yet* he had to turn in an unusually good term paper to get the grade he wanted.

Here we see that *yet* connects the two sentences in thought, though they still remain two sentences in written form. But if they are read aloud, they will sound the same, whether punctuated as one or as two sentences.

Subordinating conjunctions. The common subordinating conjunctions are these: *after, although, as, as if, as soon as, as though, because, before, if, in case that, in order that, once, provided that, since, so that, though, till, unless, until, when, where, while.**

If you put one of these at the head of a sentence, you transform that sentence into a sentence fragment called an adverbial clause. For example,

He reached the station

is a sentence. But in

After he reached the station

you have a sentence fragment that must be completed, as in

After he reached the station, he leaped from the taxi.

The subordinating conjunction both connects its clause to the rest of the sentence (even if it begins the sentence) and expresses a relationship; for

---

* Note to instructor: The subordinating conjunctions that introduce noun clauses are a partially different list. They have been omitted here because noun clauses are not a major writing problem.

example, *if* and *unless* express a condition; *in order that* and *so that* express purpose; and *since* expresses either cause or time. The adverbial clauses introduced by subordinating conjunctions are generally movable within a sentence. Examples:

If you wish, you may visit your cousin in Milwaukee.
You may, *if you wish,* visit your cousin in Milwaukee.
You may visit your cousin in Milwaukee *if you wish.*

Prepositions are words like *of, in,* and *to* which are usually followed by a noun or a personal pronoun in its object form (*me, you, him, her, it, us, them*). The unit of preposition-plus-object is called a prepositional phrase.

The English language contains about sixty prepositions. Of these the nine most frequently used are these:

1. One-syllable   at, by, for, from, in, of, on, to, with

There are four kinds other than one-syllable prepositions:

2. Two-syllable   about, against, among, before, behind, below, beneath, between, beyond, despite, except, inside, into, outside, under, upon

3. *-ing* prepositions   These consist of a verb plus the suffix *-ing:* assuming, beginning, barring, concerning, considering, during, following, including, involving, pending, regarding, succeeding (The verb stems of *during* and *pending* are not in use today.)

4. Two-word   ahead of, apart from, as for, away from, because
   prepositions   of, contrary to, due to, inside of, instead of, together with, out of, owing to, up at, up to

5. Prepositions   by dint of, by means of, by way of, in addition to,
   containing nouns   in advance of, in case of, in comparison with, in front of, in lieu of, in place of, in spite of, on account of, on behalf of, with regard to

Pronouns are a group of words, limited in number, which can occupy the positions of noun phrases, that is, modified nouns or bare nouns. The general class "pronouns" can be subdivided into at least ten groups, each with its own characteristics. For example, some pronouns have a plural form but not a possessive (*these*); some others have a possessive but not a plural (*anybody's*); still others have neither a plural nor a possessive (*nothing*). Here we shall concentrate on the two groups of most use to anyone learning to write: personal pronouns and relative pronouns. These two groups can be charted as follows:

PERSONAL PRONOUNS
Singular

	Subject	Object	Pre-Noun Possessive	Substitute Possessive
1st	I	me	my	mine
2nd	you	you	your	yours
3rd M	he	him	his	his
F	she	her	her	hers
N	it	it	its	its

Plural

	Subject	Object	Pre-Noun Possessive	Substitute Possessive
1st	we	us	our	ours
2nd	you	you	your	yours
3rd	they	them	their	theirs

RELATIVE PRONOUNS

	Subject	Object	Pre-Noun	Substitute
Sg.	who	whom	whose	whose
Pl.	who	whom	whose	whose

Some uses of personal pronouns are as follows:

1. Pronouns in the subject column are used as subjects of the verb, as in "*I* caught the rabbit" and "Jim and *I* caught the rabbit." They are also used in the position following any form of the verb *be (am, is, are, was, were, be, being, been)*, as in "This is *she*," "It must have been *they*," and "It was *I* who told *her*." Exception: "It's me" is normal Standard English; "It is I" is stiff and highly formal.
2. Pronouns in the object column are used as objects of the verb and preposition, as in "We saw Karl and *him* in the dining room" (OV), "This is between you and *me*" (OP), and "Letters were sent to Joan and *her*" (OP).
3. The pre-noun possessive *its* is spelled without the apostrophe, as in "Sarah combed *its* furry coat." The similar form with the apostrophe, *it's*, means "It is."

Some uses of relative pronouns are as follows:

1. The pronoun in the subject column, *who,* is used as the subject of the verb, as in "The girl *who* won the prize was Rachel."
2. The pronoun in the object column, *whom,* is used as the object of the verb or preposition, as in "The girl *whom* you saw is Julie's room-mate" (OV), "The girl to *whom* I spoke had a warm smile" (OP), and "The girl *whom* I spoke to had a warm smile" (OP).

Qualifiers, or intensifiers, are a set of words and phrases that occur before an adjective or adverb and increase or lessen its force.

ILLUSTRATIVE LIST OF QUALIFIERS

very weakly	*stark* naked	*a bit* tired
rather good	*brand* new	*a little* short
somewhat disturbed	*just* right	*good and* warm
quite pleasantly	*precious* little *	*kind of* dirty
real nice *	*clean* out *	*sort of* disgusted
pretty hot *	*plumb* crazy	*dead* sure *
right now *	*great* big *	*full* well *
much alive	*plenty* big	*mighty* fine *

Sometimes the open parts of speech also modify adjectives or adverbs; for example:

Noun: The journey was *miles* long.
Verb: It was *freezing* cold.
Adjective: The shirt was *dark* blue.
Adverb: You played *extremely* well.

Some qualifiers, *real* and *kind of,* for instance, are colloquial, that is, are characteristic of speech but not of writing. These should be avoided in college writing.

* These qualifiers are not adjectives but are homophones of adjectives, that is, they are pronounced and spelled the same as adjectives but have a different meaning or use.

INDEX

Classified Reference Chart